Cross-Over Bags ©

By Jeanne L. Perrine

Editor: Merle D. Perrine

Cover Design: Trilisa M. Perrine

Type Setter: Trilisa M. Perrine

Illustrator: Jeanne L. Perrine

Photographer: Trilisa M. Perrine

Proofreader: Rebecca A. Kendall

Printed by Palmer Printing
P.O. Box 1575, St. Cloud, MN 56302

ISBN 0-9777364-0-7 (previously ISBN 1-41204187-2)

www.JeannesEclecticDesigns.com

⌘ Acknowledgements
and a big Thank You to the following individuals

When I first gave consideration to stepping into the role of author, I'm sure I could hear a bit of a groan behind the grin and encouraging words offered by my husband, Merle. He proofed and edited a number of my papers while I completed nursing school. Consequently, I'm sure he knew he was about to undertake quite a task. He has done a great job in spite of my insistence on some unconventional use of grammar. Thank You. I could not have written this book without your help.

Trilisa, you have been invaluable, too. Your eye for the unusual shot has kept the photos fresh and interesting. Your computer skills are phenomenal! And your belief in me has kept me going. Thank You.

Becky, your eye for detail and the fun time spent together while you were proofreading was enjoyed and appreciated. Thank You.

There are so many people who have played a role in my writing this book: family, friends, students and even some people with whom I have had very limited contact. Vicki, Minnie, Marti, Cheryl, Kim, Joyce, Joanne, Loraine, Sharon, Kurtis, and "the two Dawns" are a few of the people who have offered encouragement and input that has been greatly appreciated. Thank You.

Judy and Jim of Judy's Quilt 'N' Sew continually offer support in so many ways. I Thank You.

Julie, Paula and her sewing friends were gracious enough to test the patterns, for which I am grateful. Some of Julie's work can be seen on page 99. Thank You.

Most of all I thank my God from whom I draw my strength and who has placed these precious and encouraging people in my life.

With Love and Thanks,

Jeanne Perrine

⌘ Table of Contents

⌘ CROSS-OVER BAGS

The leftover Moo Goo Gai Pan was carried home from the restaurant in that little white take-out box. Most people give the container no thought except that it's a time-honored symbol of Chinese food and it works well. But that night I tossed and turned all night dreaming about those little white boxes and 3-D Cross-Over bag construction. It's still unclear whether it was indigestion or possibly inspiration that kept me dreaming all night about this project. All the assembly work is flat, making these projects easy. Really. But if you do decide to use one of your creations for Oriental take-out, don't forget to line it with foil!

Many of the projects in this book have techniques in common. These procedures will be written out in a special section. When a particular technique is needed in a project, the name and page will be referenced, thereby allowing more space for additional projects in the book. After you have made a couple of the bags, it will be unnecessary to refer to these pages again. It is important, however, to read the *General Information Pages*, which give you tips on how to be successful with your project construction.

The supply list at the beginning of each project is specific to that project. The *Basic Supplies* are listed and addressed at the beginning of the book. It is suggested you read this section **prior to starting** a project.

I hope you enjoy making these projects as much as I've enjoyed designing them. They were designed to bring out the creator/designer in you. Whether you want something fun, sassy, sophisticated, elegant or whimsical, you make your own statement with them. So, make that statement and please feel free to send me photos. My contact information can be found at: www.JeannesEclecticDesigns.com I'd love to see them!
Have fun creating! *Jeanne Perrine*

⌘ Basic Supplies

⌘ Fabrics

The most fun and the most visible personal choices you will make creating these bags are the fabrics and threads. All of the samples in this book are made of good quality tightly woven 100% cotton fabrics. I would recommend experimenting with other fabrics only after making a couple of these projects with cotton. It will help you understand more clearly the changes needed when using other fabrics. The major problem encountered when using synthetic fabrics is the heat required for fusing. Lowering the iron temperature and increasing the time for fusing is all that is actually required. It can be done but very carefully.

It's best to have some unifying element in each project, whether it is color, theme or design. Bright and wild to soft and soothing are all great choices. But don't hesitate to use your imagination! It is important to note that if you are using fabric that requires matching the design you may need to purchase extra yardage. The extent of extra fabric needed is dependent upon the size of the print. However, yardage used in this book is figured with directional fabric in mind and that the fabric has 42 inches of usable fabric from selvage to selvage.

⌘ Threads

Thread can make or break your project. (Pun intended.) Although I like the beautiful sheen a satin stitch gives with 40-weight rayon embroidery thread, it is not as strong and durable as polyester threads. There are some new poly threads that have a beautiful sheen and offer better durability. Poly threads are the strongest and most resistant to abrasion. They may be the best choice for larger bags or bags that will get a great deal of use. Quality is the most important factor in the choice of thread you use. Remember thread does have a shelf life. Most of the projects in this book will require a large spool or two small spools of thread.

Thread choice is also an important part of your design statement in these bags. Solids or variegated threads work well. Try contrasting threads. If you're uncomfortable in making that decision try laying a thin piece of solid fabric in a contrasting color on the edge of your cut pattern pieces to see what the effect would be. You may be pleasantly surprised at how much it adds to the final project.

I always use the same thread in the bobbin as I do in the top of the machine. If you choose to have a different thread in the bobbin, you will find it necessary to constantly check the tension and keep it very finely tuned. Whatever your choices, I would recommend that you try running a satin stitch on a scrap of textile sandwich before using something too unusual such as metallic thread. Keep in mind that metallic thread is not very strong. If in doubt, try it out.

⌘ Stabilizers

There are many stabilizers available to choose from. All of the projects in this book have been made with Timtex™. It is a delightful, lightweight, 1/8 inch thick rayon and polyester blend interfacing. It is strong and holds its' shape well. There is no need to be concerned about the grain of the Timtex™. Pieces may be cut in any direction. Wrinkles can be ironed out at any time unless you have ironed in a crease. If you need to iron the Timtex™ before sandwiching, it is important to cover it with a pressing cloth or a piece of muslin. The fact that Timtex™ can be ironed at any point is important because some of these projects are quite large. You will need to roll some pieces in order to fit them through the machine opening. Some projects will also need to be a bit distorted during the assembly process because they are quite small. None of this is a problem as you can press them at any time. If you enjoy special stitching or quilting, most thick stabilizers will accommodate the decorative stitching well. Extra stitching is not needed as a functional part of any of the creations in this book. Timtex™ can be purchased by the yard at a width of 22". You can also purchase it prepackaged at 13 ½" x 22". There are a number of new thick stabilizers on the market now. Keep an eye out for them. Try them and let me know how they work for you. I have found that the thicker and firmer the stabilizer used in these projects the happier I am with the results.

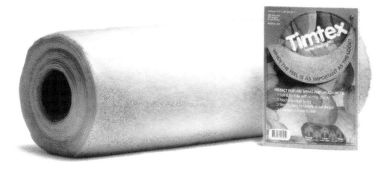

⌘ Fusible Web

If you have a favorite fusible web, feel free to use it. All the instructions have been written with Steam-A-Seam 2® (S-A-S 2) in mind. If you have done any quilting you are familiar with the term "sandwich". It is simply the layering of textiles. Fusible web is the glue that holds it all together. There is no need for quilting except as a design element. I have chosen Steam-A-Seam 2® for these projects for a number of reasons. First, I like the idea that I can rectify a mistake at any time before ironing. (I do make mistakes.) Simply lift the S-A-S 2 and fabric and reposition it any time before ironing. Piecing it is also very easy so there is never any waste. Just save all those scraps! Steam-A-Seam 2® comes in packages and also by the yard. It can be purchased in three widths : 12", 18" and 24". Be sure to read the patterns well to see which width was used and adjust accordingly if you are unable to purchase the recommended width. Another benefit I prefer is that it adds just a bit of firmness without becoming stiff. And, last but not least, I find it doesn't gum up my needle as quickly as some of the others. If you have trouble with the needle gumming up, the problem is that you have not allowed enough time for the fusing to be complete. There is no need to be concerned about overheating S-A-S 2; it doesn't lose its bonding properties if you iron longer than the recommended time. Steam-A-Seam 2® is a two-sided fusible web that has paper on both sides. DO NOT iron it with the paper on. (This is different than all other fusible webs.) If you

choose to use a different fusible web be sure to adjust your patterns accordingly and follow the manufacturer's instructions carefully. All fusible webs will eventually gum up your needle to some degree; some will more than others. Using a new needle for each project is important. However, if it's only a matter of the needle being gummed up, use a little Tri-Flow™ on a piece of scrap fabric and run it up and down the needle. This will clean the needle well. Be sure to turn off your sewing machine before cleaning the needle. Check with the dealership if you have any concern about using Tri-Flow™ with your machine. This technique works well.

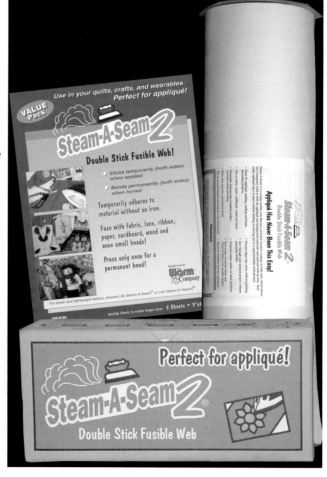

⌘ Cutting Tools

What would we ever do if we had to go back to cutting everything out with scissors? The rotary cutting system has decreased cutting time and increased accuracy for most of us. When I do need to cut anything with scissors I make sure that I use a good quality very sharp pair. Sharp points allow for precision cutting of holes in the sandwich for eyelets, grommets or other handle applications.

Rotary cutting is great but safety is a necessity in using the system. Think of rotary cutters as round razor blades. If you have children or pets, you should get in the habit of always closing the cutter each time you use it. There are wonderful cutters now available that close when you release the hand pressure. My favorite is the Omnigrid® rotary cutter that is pressure sensitive. When pressure is released the blade retracts. This type of rotary cutter is great not only for safety but also for the sake of your fabric. I have seen many students lay an open cutter on a piece of just cut fabric and nick a hole in the fabric with the open cutter. They were not happy campers! The first cutter to purchase is the 45mm size. I use it most of the time.

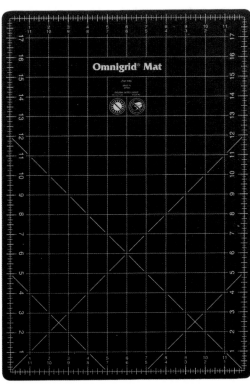

A cutting mat 17" x 24" is the smallest I would recommend purchasing. It is easy to carry to class and large enough for most projects. If you can invest in a larger one to leave out at home, it is very nice to have.

⌘ Acrylic Rulers

 The three rulers I use most frequently are the 12-1/2" square, 6" x 12" and the
8-1/2" x 24". I personally like Omnigrip™ rulers best. They grip the textile being cut;
therefore, you experience less slipping. For me the bright green markings are
easy to read. There are many brands and all of them will work.

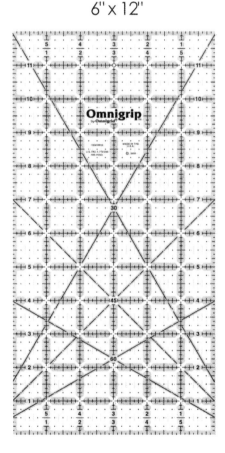

6" x 12"

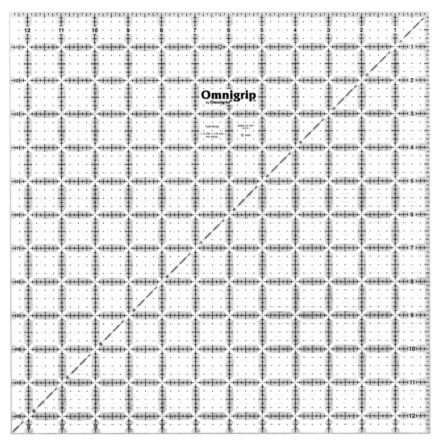

12-1/2" Square

⌘ Marking Tools

These projects often require marking. Some of the marks need to be erasable.
I like a small clear line for accuracy. Be sure to remove the markings before
ironing as they may be difficult to remove after heat is applied. You may have a
favorite marker. All of them are fine if they are easily removable.

⌘ Iron and Ironing Surface

A steam iron is needed in all of these projects. When using fusible web, no matter how careful you are, it seems some of the melted web adheres to the iron and the ironing surface. I cover my board with a layer or two of inexpensive muslin. I also have a hot iron cleaner handy. Just follow the instructions on the package. There are a number of good iron cleaners available.

⌘ Sewing Machine, Feet and Needles

Be sure your machine is in good working order and that you are familiar with the tension settings on your machine. You may need to adjust the tensions. You can make these projects using only a zigzag stitch but you will have a more "finished" look with a satin stitch. Unless otherwise stated I use a Microtex 60/8 or 70/10 sharp needle. These needles leave only a very small hole. Frequent needle changes are important. It is best to change the needle every project or two depending on the size of the project. A good rule of thumb is to change your needle every 8 hours of use. The open toe zigzag foot is the main foot used with all of these projects. A zipper foot will be needed if the project has a zippered pocket. If you choose to do some decorative quilting you should also have a darning foot.

⌘ Templates

Most of the pieces in these projects require only the use of an acrylic ruler and cutting to the required dimensions. However, most projects will also require a flap pattern piece. These will be printed at actual size within the project instructions or the page number where the pattern piece can be found will be noted. They will be labeled with a pattern designation letter and the letter "R". The R indicates the need to use the reverse of the printed pattern piece. I encourage you to photocopy the pattern pieces and trace them onto template plastic. Cut them out, mark the pattern letter on each one and save them for the next time you want to make the project.

⌘ Techniques

For those who haven't worked with these techniques before, it is important to read this section carefully before starting a project. Each project will reference the technique by page number, making it easier to address the specific technique in question should you need to refer to the instructions while working on a project.

⌘ Chart Usage

The charts have been set up as a quick guide to cutting. It is important to realize that each pattern is written with directional fabric in mind. However, additional fabric may be required if you are matching the print on the fabric design.

The first chart in each project requires a cut measurement from selvage to selvage. The exception is Steam-A-Seam 2® (S-A-S 2) which will at times be cut with the length of the roll. There are also occasions when a layout diagram will be provided. The small projects can often be cut from scraps.

The second chart is generally a cut with the lengthwise grain of the fabrics. The pieces in chart 2 are oversized pattern pieces. It is very important to cut these pieces oversized. Stack the pieces together according to piece size. There should be five (5) layers of each pattern piece: one (1) of Timtex™, two (2) of S-A-S 2 and two (2) of fabric. It is also helpful to label them.

The third chart gives the final dimensions of each pattern piece. Cutting the sandwich down from the oversized cut provides a clean crisp edge. This crisp edge allows for the best results on the satin stitched seams. Handle the edges as little as possible so as not to fray the edges.

⌘ Templates

Most pieces for the majority of the projects in this book are cut using measurements only. However, there are a number of pieces that require a pattern piece. It is best to make a template from template plastic. I use two rotary cutters. One is used only for fabric and one is specifically designated for paper and plastic.

The straight edges of the pattern pieces are best cut using a ruler and rotary cutter. Photo copy the pattern pieces and lay the template plastic over the copy. Three (3) pattern pieces (I, J and L) will require taping. The pieces with a dotted line across them need to be aligned at that spot and taped before cutting. Cut the piece out using the rotary cutting system. Transfer the letters and markings from the photocopy to the newly made template. The "R" on the pattern pieces simply indicates that the pattern piece will be used in reverse. There is no need to cut two templates. Simply turn over the template and use the reverse side.

I usually store all my templates in a plastic bag taped to the inside back cover of my book for use at a later date. Then I never have to remake them or look for them again.

⌘ Marking

Just a general word or two about marking will be sufficient. When marking any line using a ruler be sure to allow for the space the marking implement will occupy. Many times when making a satin stitched seam by butting two sandwich pieces together, it is difficult to see where the seam comes together while stitching. Marking a chalk line along the edge of the seam may be helpful as it will provide a visual guideline. Marking a guide for cutting holes in the textile sandwich for eyelet or grommet insertion can be done with a pen or pencil as the mark will be completely removed when the hole is cut.

⌘ Cutting

The assumption is that the fabric being used has 42 inches of usable fabric from selvage to selvage. It is also assumed that the individual understands how to square the fabric, remove the selvages and use the rotary cutting system. There is no need to consider the grain of either Timtex™ or S-A-S 2. All pattern pieces can easily be cut with the rotary cutting system except for the rounded corners of the credit card holder and the thumb notch on its vinyl inserts. Scissors will also be required to cut holes in the sandwich for eyelet or grommet insertion. Although the layouts of projects consider the grain of the fabrics, don't let that stifle your creativity. Cut your fabrics in the direction that best suits the design of the fabric and the bag. Realize that you may need more fabric. Cutting the fabric on the bias creates more stretch. The tendency to stretch the fabric will be most noticed in the sandwiching process when ironing. Be careful to control the fabric at that time.

Some of the patterns require large cuts. Two rulers can be used together if you do not have the proper size ruler. (see picture) While lining up the two rulers for measuring be sure to use the longest possible edge of the first ruler along the side opposite the cutting line. Butt the rulers together. When you are confident of the measurement, hold the second ruler firmly in place while cutting. As long as the second ruler is firmly held in place, movement of the first ruler should be of no concern (see picture).

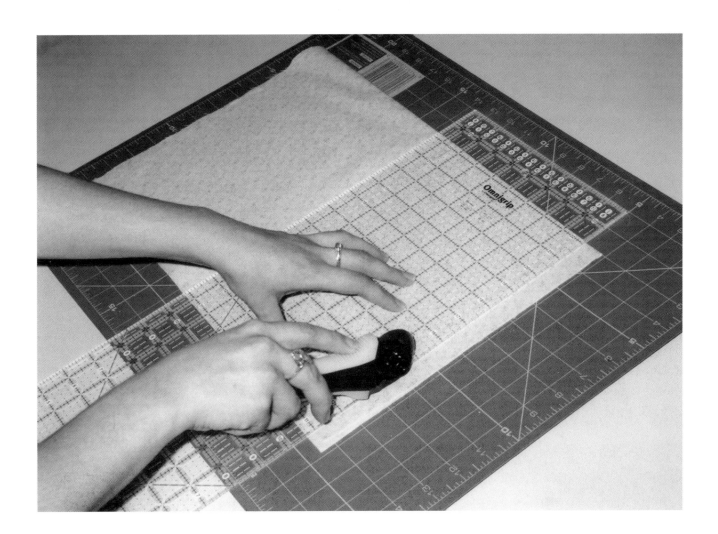

Hand position is important when holding the ruler in place. Laying your hand flat on the ruler is not the advisable position. The ruler is more likely to slip while you are cutting with the flat hand position. Having the hand in a "tented" position (see picture) gives you the best control. This "tented" position allows you to "spider" walk your hand along the length of the ruler while you are cutting. Don't try to walk your hand up the ruler while there is any pressure on the edge of the ruler from the rotary cutter. Although this tip seems elementary, it is the one error I see most frequently with beginning students. After the cut is complete, lay the cutter to the side and without releasing pressure on the ruler, gently move the newly cut fabric away from the ruler. This allows you the opportunity of being sure the cut was complete and didn't leave any little uncut threads. Don't run the cutter back and forth over any uncut areas that did not get cut on the first try. Simply cut in one direction (preferably away from your body) again to finish the cut. Running the rotary cutter back and forth across the fabric or sandwich will always give you an unsightly frayed edge which will be much more difficult with which to work.

⌘ Sandwiching

Sandwiching is simply a term used to denote the layering of textiles. Making a sandwich in this book will always refer to five (5) layers of textiles unless otherwise stated. These layers consist of Timtex™ in the center with S-A-S 2 on each side and then fabric ironed in place on each side of the S-A-S 2. There will be times when you are directed to sandwich only one side of the Timtex™. This is done in order to allow for some application that needs to be finished before the second layer of fabric is applied such as a pocket sewn in or a magnetic clasp installed. The second layer of S-A-S 2 and fabric is then applied in the same manner as the first layer.

There are a number of tips that can make the process of sandwiching successful. First, it is important that the Timtex™ is flat. If it needs to be pressed, use a pressing cloth or place an inexpensive piece of muslin over the Timtex™ before ironing it. Secondly, it is also important to have your fabric free of wrinkles. And last, but very importantly, be sure to take the time needed to fully fuse the fabric to the Timtex™.

The instructions in this book have been written with the use of S-A-S 2 in mind. Other fusible webs can be used. Be sure to adapt the instructions to the choice of fusible web and follow the manufactures instructions carefully. Overheating can happen with some fusible web products. Remember, Do Not iron S-A-S 2 with the protective paper in place. Only iron the fabric in place once you are fully satisfied with the placement of the fabric. This is one of the main reasons I choose to work with S-A-S 2. It allows me to remove and reposition as many times as needed. This becomes important if I am placing an embroidery design in a specific place on the pattern piece. Embroidery needs to be done before the sandwiching process.

Steam is important to the fusing process. However, very hot bursts of steam can cause the Timtex™ to dimple the sandwich. Because you are working with cotton and a synthetic, Timtex™, the approach should be tailored slightly. Set the iron to the low steam setting. If the iron being used does not have that capability, iron without steam and use a spray bottle to lightly spritz the sandwich with water before ironing. S-A-S 2 does not lose its fusing properties from ironing too long as some fusible webs do. Therefore, be sure to iron until the fusing process is complete.

The layering process with S-A-S 2 is as follows. First, remove one side of the paper and place the sticky side on the Timtex™. Then remove the second piece of paper and position the fabric. The fabric can be repositioned as many times as needed before ironing. Lastly, iron the sandwich until the fusing process is complete. This can be tested by gently lifting the edge of the fabric after cooling and if it doesn't easily separate, the fusing is complete. I layer and fuse one side of the sandwich at a time. Iron the sandwich from the center of the piece out to the edges. This will allow you to lift and reposition the fabric if a wrinkle starts to form. Wrinkles would indicate that the fabric is probably being stretched. Be careful when ironing not to push the iron hard over the fabric especially if the fabric has been cut on the bias.

To avoid getting fusible web on the iron I tend to cut my fusible web on the slight side of the given measurement and the fabric on the larger side of the given measurement. Iron at the highest temperature appropriate for the fabric. The lower the temperature, the longer the ironing time should be to allow the fusing process to have its full effect.

Piecing S-A-S 2 is easy and will not cause any problems such as lines or distortion in the final project. Simply overlap the edges of S-A-S 2 when piecing and continue on with the instructions as if it were a single piece of fusible web.

The question is often asked, "Why are the pieces for the sandwich cut larger than the final pattern pieces?" There are a number of advantages to making the sandwich a bit larger and cutting it down to the final dimensions. Layering and lining up five (5) different pieces of textile perfectly is difficult at best, if not impossible. Cutting the sandwich down to the final dimension gives a clean crisp edge to the piece. The crisp edge is important because the satin stitched edges look best when all five (5) layers are exactly the same. Handle the edges as little as possible after the final trim has been done. Excessive handling can cause some fraying of the fabric. If that occurs be sure to snip the frayed threads before satin stitching. This will give the most finished and professional look to the end product.

⌘ Stitching

There are a number of different types of stitches called for throughout this book. The following will explain how and when the different stitches are to be used.

Two related ideas are embroidery and quilting. Embroidery should be done before sandwiching. Quilting, although not needed structurally, adds a little extra punch to any bag. Quilting should be done just before starting the Cross-Over Construction phase of the bag.

⌘ Satin Stitching

The "satin stitch" is the basic stitch used in all of the projects in this book. A very close zigzag stitch can be used if your machine does not have a satin stitch setting. It has a flat side and a more rounded side. When stitching the bag, it is best to stitch with the outside of the bag facing up. This is the side of the satin stitch that will be rounded. Use a scrap of excess sandwich or a piece of Timex™ to check the tension balance of the satin stitch before starting to stitch on the actual bag pieces. It is also important to check the edges of your sandwich pieces to be sure there are no loose threads. If there are, clip them before you begin stitching. It is highly recommended that each satin stitch seam be stitched twice. The first satin stitch seam should be sewn at a setting of 0.3mm length and a 4.0mm width. When stitching over the seam the second time the settings should be 0.3mm length and a 6.0mm width. There is no need to lock stitch any seam if it will be sewn over by another seam. It is always better, however, to lock stitch if you have any question. When using the satin stitch to join two (2) pieces together it is important to be sure the seam is perfectly centered over the edges of both pieces.

Satin stitching the edges of the sandwich pieces takes a little time to do well but it will make your project look professional. The needle should fall just off the right side edge of the textile sandwich. Like the satin stitch used to join two (2) pieces, stitch at 0.3 mm length and 4.0 mm width the first time around and 0.3 mm length and 6.0 mm width the second time. When turning at the corners, stop with the needle down in the right position off the edge of the sandwich and pivot. Butt the sandwich up to the needle and continue to stitch. A little practice on some scraps is always a good plan.

⌘ Lock Stitch

"Lock stitch," "tack stitch" or "fix" are all the same thing. It's simply a way of making a knot. If your machine doesn't have a button to press to make a knot, simply set the machine as close to "zero" (0) as possible while in the straight stitch mode and take a few stitches. Then clip the threads as close to the surface as possible.

⌘ Backstitching

"Backstitching" is another way to be sure a seam is secure. Most machines have a reverse button making it simple to backstitch by pressing the button and allowing the machine to backstitch. The backstitch is used on the vinyl inserts at both ends of the seam. It's also used when stitching in the ditch to secure the tops of the bags.

⌘ Stitching in the Ditch

This is the simple technique of straight stitching in the valley of a seam. It is used as a part of the 3-D Cross-Over Construction. Stitching in the ditch adds strength and stability to the bag. Always backstitch at the beginning and at the end of these seams.

⌘ Cross-Over Construction A and B

Cross-Over Construction is a simple but strong way of turning the flat project into a three-dimensional (3-D) creation. If the project has become wrinkled in the process of working with it, now is a good time to iron out the entire piece. Refer to the "A" drawing below and the associated "A" instructions for the Lunch Bag or Great Gift Bag. All other projects in this book are made using instructions "B" and refer to the drawing labeled "B".

⌘ Step 1

Position the project interior side up. Fold and finger press the Flap seams in toward the (A) Front and Back or (B) Sides. Fold and finger press the Side, Front and Back seams in toward the bottom.

A.

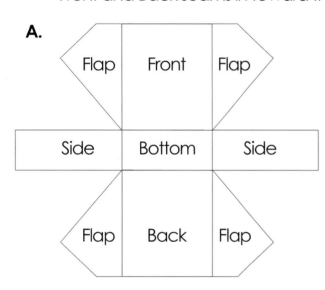

B.

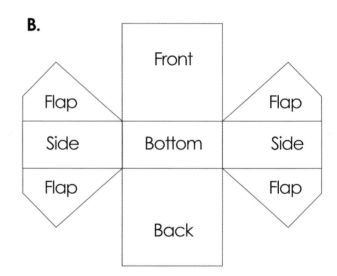

⌘ Step 2

Fold the Front, Back and Sides up to form a box. Bring the Flaps over the (A) Front and Back or (B) Sides. Push straight pins through at five (5) points. (see drawing)

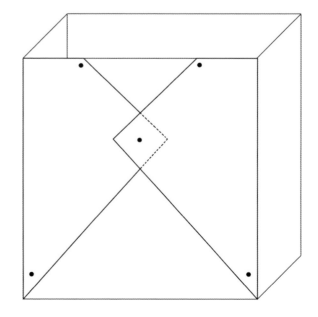

Be sure the tops of the Flaps line up straight with the tops of the (A) Sides or (B) Front and Back.

⌘ Step 3

Stitch in the ditch along the tops of all four (4) of the Flaps. (see drawing)

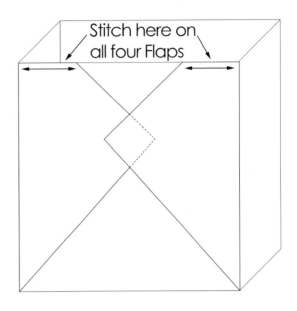

Stitch here on all four Flaps

⌘ Step 4

Look at the satin stitching on your Flaps and bring the Flap with the best stitching to the outside. It doesn't matter which Flap is forward.

⌘ Step 5

Apply liquid fabric glue all along the underside of the Flaps. Do not use a glue stick. Make sure the Flaps lay flat and that the corners at the bottom don't gap. Press pins through the entire thickness at the five (5) previously pinned points. Leave the pins in place until the glue is completely dry. Remove the pins.

⌘ Step 6

Slip the project over the end of the ironing board or a piece of wood and iron out any wrinkles before going on to embellish the bag.

⌘ Evening Take-Out Bag

Approximately 5-1/2" x 5-1/2" x 4-7/8"

Make one of these fashionable bags to go with your favorite evening attire and take it out on the town! Please note there are two versions of this bag in the following set of instructions. Refer to the photo gallery to view the blue and red bag styles. The only differences are the handle and handle attachments.

⌘ Supply List:

Basic Supplies
Timtex ™: 2/3 yards
18" Steam-A-Seam 2®
   (S-A-S 2): 1-3/8 yards
Fabric 1 (exterior): 3/8 yard
Fabric 2 (interior): 3/8 yard
Fabric 3 (accent): 1/8 yard
Thread to coordinate
   or contrast
Magnetic Snap: 1 set
Eyelets: (2) 1/4" sets
Fabric Glue: your favorite liquid
   fabric adhesive

Buttons: 1 for the blue bag -OR-
   3 for the red bag (They need to
   be large enough to cover the
   magnetic snap for both bags
   and large enough to cover the
   eyelets on the handle
   attachment for the red bag. You
   may want to wait until your bag
   is finished to select the buttons.)
Handles: 12" chain with at least a
   3/8" deep clasp for the blue bag,
   -OR- 20" of 16/32" cotton piping
   cord for the red bag.

✂ Step 1. Cutting (see page 18)

Make templates (see page 16) for the pattern pieces A, B, C, D, E and F from template plastic and mark it with the pattern letter. You will not need to cut any of the Handle tabs (F) if you are making the red bag. Stack the pieces as you cut them. Each stack should contain: (1) template (except for the Top and Bottom pieces), (1) piece of Timtex™, (2) pieces of S-A-S 2 and (2) pieces of fabric. All pieces within the stack should have the same approximate dimensions.

Chart 1

Item	#	Size
Timtex™	3	6" x 22"
	1	4-3/4" x 22"
18" S-A-S 2	6	18" x 6"
	1	18" x 5-1/4"
	1	18" x 4-3/4"
Fabric 1	2	42" x 6"
Fabric 2	2	42" x 6"

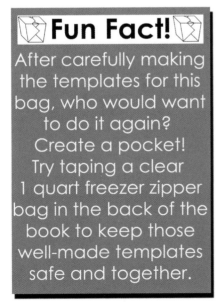

🗋 Fun Fact! 🗋

After carefully making the templates for this bag, who would want to do it again? Create a pocket! Try taping a clear 1 quart freezer zipper bag in the back of the book to keep those well-made templates safe and together.

Chart 2

Item	#	Size
Timtex™		
Front and Back (A)	2	6" x 6"
Top	1	6" x 5-1/2"
Side Flaps (C)	1	6" x 16"
Front Closing Flap (D)	1	6" x 3-1/2"
Sides (B)	2	6" x 5-1/4"
Top Inner Folding Flaps (E)	2	5-1/4" x 3-1/4"
Bottom	1	4-3/4" x 4"
Handle Tabs (F)	2	3-3/4" x 2"
S-A-S 2		
Front and Back (A)	4	6" x 6"
Top	2	6" x 5-1/2"
Side Flaps (C)	2	6" x 16"
Front Closing Flap (D)	2	6" x 3-1/2"
Sides (B)	4	6" x 5-1/4"
Top Inner Folding Flaps (E)	4	5-1/4" x 3-1/4"
Bottom	2	4-3/4" x 4"
Handle Tabs (F)	4	3-3/4" x 2"
Fabric 1		
Front and Back (A)	2	6" x 6"
Top	1	6" x 5-1/2"
Front Closing Flap (D)	1	6" x 3-1/2"
Sides (B)	2	6" x 5-1/4"
Side Flaps (C)	2	6" x 16"
Top Inner Folding Flaps (E)	2	5-1/4" x 3-1/4"
Fabric 2		
Front and Back (A)	2	6" x 6"
Top	1	6" x 5-1/2"
Front Closing Flap (D)	1	6" x 3-1/2"
Sides (B)	2	6" x 5-1/4"
Top Inner Folding Flaps (E)	2	5-1/4" x 3-1/4"
Fabric 3		
Bottom	2	4-3/4" x 4"
Handle Tabs (F)	2	3-3/4" x 2"

⌘ Step 2. Sandwiching
(see page 20)

Each piece of Timtex™ needs S-A-S 2 and fabric on each side. All pieces will have Fabric 1 on one side and Fabric 2 on the other side. The exception is the Bottom piece and the Handle Tabs (F) which will have fabric 3 on both sides. Be sure to steam iron each side of the sandwich until the fusing process is complete.

✂ Step 3. Recutting

Using your templates trim the pieces down to the exact sizes indicated. **Do Not Forget** the Flaps need special attention. Two pieces need to be cut as template C and 2 pieces need to be cut as C-R, the reverse of template C (see drawing).

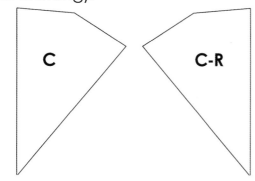

Chart 3

Item	#	Size
Front & Back	2	A
Top	1	5-1/2" x 4-7/8"
Side Flaps	2	C
Side Flaps	2	C-R
Front Closing Flap	1	D
Sides	2	B
Top Inner Folding Flaps	2	E
Bottom	1	4-1/4" x 3-1/2"
Handle Tabs	2	F

⌘ Step 4. Satin Stitch
(see page 22)

The exterior fabric should be facing up throughout this step.

- Satin stitch completely around the Handle Tabs (F) and set them aside.

- Satin stitch the Front Closing Flap (D) to the Top (5-1/2" x 4-7/8"). To this unit satin stitch the Back (A). Next satin stitch the Bottom (4-1/4" x 3-1/2") piece to the strip. To this long unit satin stitch the Front (A). (see drawing) Satin stitch completely around the outer edges of this unit and set it aside.

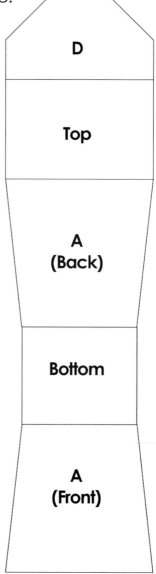

- Satin stitch one Top Inner Folding Flap (E) to one Side (B) piece. Satin stitch to this unit the Flaps (C & C-R), one on each side, making sure the top of the Flaps line up perfectly with the top of the Side (B) piece (see drawing). Satin stitch completely around this unit except the bottom of the Side piece. Repeat this process with the other side. Set these units aside.

⌘ Step 5. Preparing the Handle Tabs (F)

If you are making the red bag, skip this step. Install the eyelets (see page 85) so that the center of the hole is 1/2" below the top edge of the Handle Tabs (F). With a Handle Tab (F) centered on the Side piece (B), satin stitch it in place 1" above the seam line joining the Side (B) to the Top Inner Folding Flaps (E). Repeat this process on the other side. When the bag is finished, clip the chain clasps into the eyelets.

E

B
(Side)

C

C-R

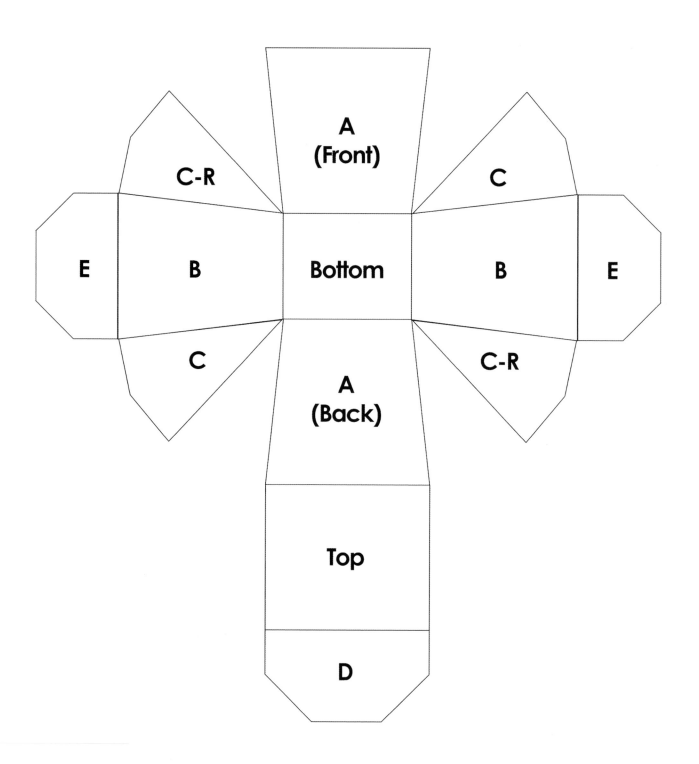

A
(Front)

C-R

C

E

B

Bottom

B

E

C

C-R

A
(Back)

Top

D

⌘ Step 6. Satin Stitch
(see page 22)

With exterior fabric facing up, satin stitch the side units to the bottom (see drawing). Satin stitch once completely around the bottom after the sides have both been joined.

⌘ Step 7. Making the Scrunchie Handle

If you are making the blue bag, skip this step. Using Fabric 1 cut a 2-1/8" strip the full width of the fabric (2-1/8" x 45"). DO NOT cut off the salvage; this will give you a strong finished edge. Fold the fabric in half lengthwise, with right sides facing each other. Sew the raw edges together with a 1/4" seam. Turn tube right side out. Using tape, wrap the ends of the 16/32" piping cord tightly. Pull the cord through the tube of fabric, using a safety pin. Straight stitch across the end of the cord several times 1/2" above the end of the tape. Cut the tape off allowing the cord to fray below the straight stitching. Flatten the cord and pull it back inside the tube of fabric so that the frayed edges of cord are just inside the fabric tube. Straight stitch across the end of the tube closing the tube. Straight stitch 1/2" above the end of the tube. This should fall over the straight stitching you did on the cord before closing the tube. Set this aside and continue on with the following instructions. Placement for the eyelet/grommet is centered on the side 1-3/4" down from the Flap (E)/Side seam.

⌘ Step 8. Cross-Over Construction B (see page 24)

-Follow the instructions carefully on Cross-Over construction B (see page 24).

-Follow the instructions on how to install the scrunchie handle (see page 88).

-Follow the instructions on magnetic clasp insertion (see page 90).

-Follow the instructions on how to attach the buttons on the bag (see page 92).

A
(Front & Back)

B
(Side)

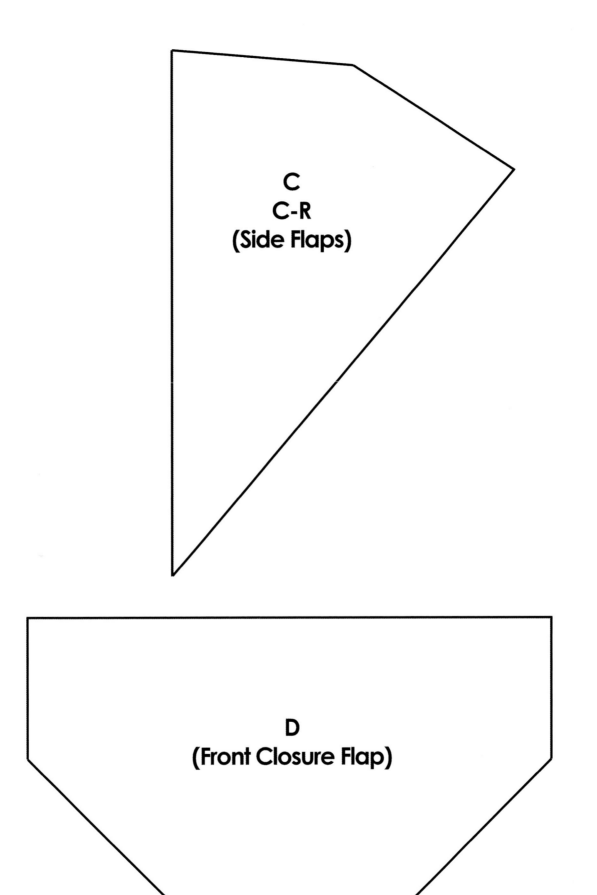

C
C-R
(Side Flaps)

D
(Front Closure Flap)

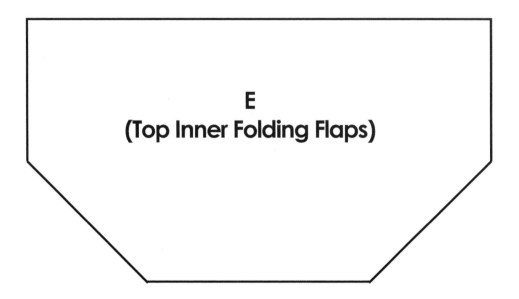

E
(Top Inner Folding Flaps)

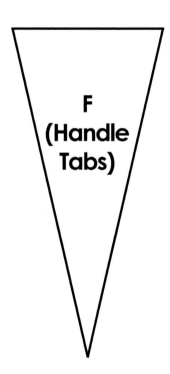

F
(Handle Tabs)

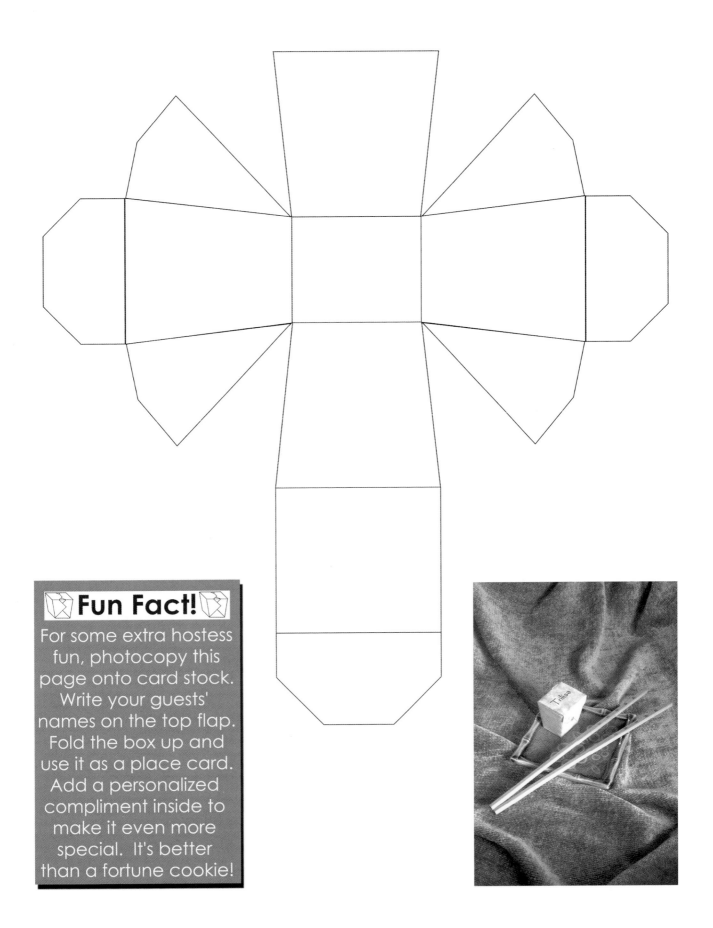

⌘ Music Bag

12-1/2" x 12" x 2"

Carry that sheet music in style! Even if you don't have enough time to practice, the bag will look great!

⌘ Supply List:

Basic Supplies
Timtex™: 1-5/8 yards
18" Steam-A-Seam 2® (S-A-S 2): 3-3/8 yard
Fabric 1 (exterior): 3/8 yard
Fabric 2 (interior): 3/8 yard
Fabric 3 (flaps): 3/4 yard
Chain (3/8"): 1-1/4 yard
Grommets (3/8"): 4 sets *
Music Embellishments: 2
Fabric Glue: your favorite liquid fabric adhesive
Thread to coordinate or contrast
   *Be sure the chain you choose will fit through the eyelets/grommets.
   You can always change the size of the eyelets/grommets used.

✄ Step 1. Cutting (see page 18)

Stack the pieces as you cut them. Each stack should contain (1) piece of Timtex™, (2) pieces of fabric and (2) pieces of S-A-S 2. All pieces within each stack should have the same dimensions. Make a template (see page 16) for the Flaps (pattern piece L on page 40) from template plastic and mark it with the pattern letter. In Chart 1 & 2 cut the Flap pieces of the Timtex™ and S-A-S 2 first.

Chart 1

Item	#	Size
Timtex™	2	12-3/4" x 22"
	1	29-1/4" x 22"
18" S-A-S 2	1	12-3/4" x 120-1/2"
Fabric 1	1	12-3/4" x 45"
Fabric 2	1	12-3/4" x 45"
Fabric 3	2	12-3/4" x 29-1/4"

Chart 2

Item	#	Size
Timtex™		
Front & Back	2	12-3/4" x 12-1/4"
Bottom	1	12-1/4" x 2-1/4"
Sides	2	12-3/4" x 2-1/4"
Flaps	1	12-3/4" x 29-1/4"
S-A-S 2		
Front & Back	4	12-3/4" x 12-1/4"
Bottom	2	12-1/4" x 2-1/4"
Sides	4	12-3/4" x 2-1/4"
Flaps	2	12-3/4" x 29-1/4"
Fabric 1		
Front & Back	2	12-3/4" x 12-1/4"
Bottom	1	12-1/4" x 2-1/4"
Sides	2	12-3/4" x 2-1/4"
Fabric 2		
Front & Back	2	12-3/4" x 12-1/4"
Bottom	1	12-1/4" x 2-1/4"
Sides	2	12-3/4" x 2-1/4"
Fabric 3		
Flaps	2	29-1/4" x 12-3/4"

⌘ Step 2. Sandwiching
(see page 20)

For the Front, Back, Bottom and Sides, you will need to have S-A-S 2, and Fabric 1 on one side of the Timtex™ and S-A-S 2 and Fabric 2 on the other side. For the Flaps you will need to have S-A-S 2 and Fabric 3 on both sides of the Timtex™. Be sure to steam iron each side of the sandwich until the fusing process is complete.

✄ Step 3. Recutting

Trim the sandwich pieces down to the following exact sizes.

Chart 3

Item	#	Size
Front & Back	2	12-1/2" x 12"
Bottom	1	12" x 2"
Sides	2	12-1/2" x 2"
Flaps	2	L
Flaps	2	L-R

⌘ Step 4. Satin Stitch

- Satin stitch (see page 22) the sides and top of the Front and Back pieces.

- Satin stitch the Front and Back pieces to the Bottom piece along the 12" side. You need only stitch one time for now. Be sure to center the seam between the two pieces while joining them together. Set this unit aside for the time being.

- Satin stitch the Flaps to the Sides. Be sure the tops line up perfectly as this will provide for a smooth finish. If you intend to satin stitch your seams a second time, now is the time.

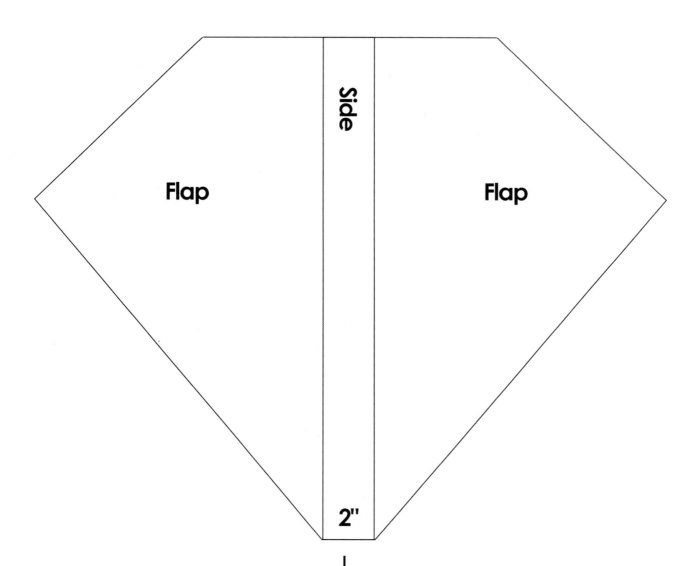

Flap

Side

Flap

2"

- Satin stitch around the entire edge of these newly joined units except for the 2" bottom of the Sides (see drawing).

- Satin stitch these units to the sides of the Bottom.

- With exterior fabric facing up, satin stitch around the entire bottom. You will need to roll the large pieces in order to fit them through the machine opening. This will not hurt your project as you can iron the entire bag after you are done stitching.

🎵 Fun Fact! 🎵

If you get glue on parts of the fabric you hadn't intended to, remove as much of it as possible with a thin piece of cardboard. Then place a piece of brown paper bag over the spot and iron it with a hot iron. The glue usually lifts off the fabric as you remove the paper.

⌘ Step 5. Cross-Over Construction B (see page 24)

Follow the instructions carefully for construction B.

⌘ Step 6. Embellishments
(see page 91)

This is the time to press your bag. Place a block of wood into the bag to press the sides more crisply. Another option is to slide the bag onto the end of the ironing board and use the side of the ironing board to press the sides of the bag. You can place anything you like at the "V" on the outside of the bag. The treble clef signatures are iron on pieces I found in a fabric store. I found they stayed better if I glued them on rather than depending on the iron on technique. Be creative and add anything fun!

⌘ Step 7. Handle Attachment
(see page 85)

Follow the instructions on eyelet/grommet and chain installation. The grommets are placed on the Front and Back of the bag equidistant from the center. Place them near the top and through the Flaps. I prefer them near the upper angle as shown in the picture.

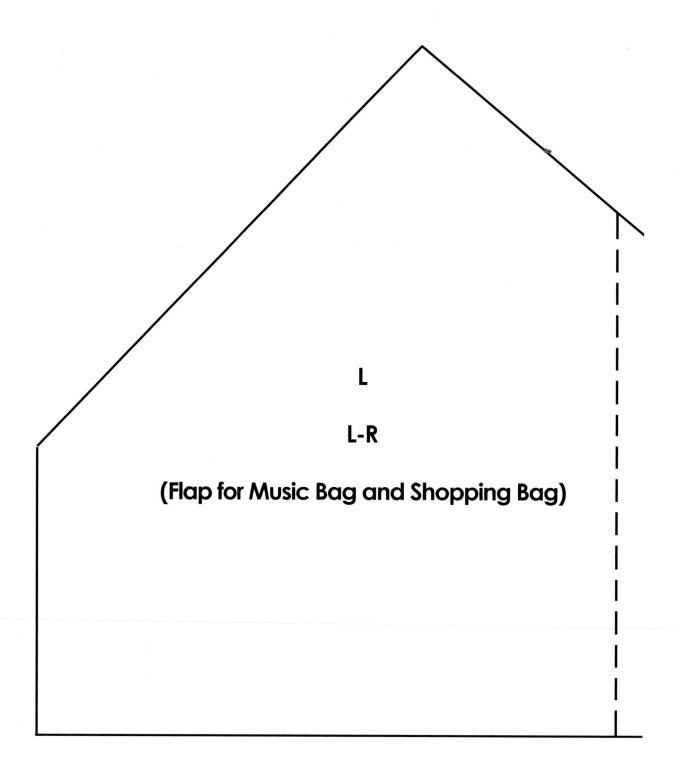

L

L-R

(Flap for Music Bag and Shopping Bag)

-Photocopy both pages.

-Tape them together at the dotted line before making your template. Be sure to label the template with the appropriate letters.

⌘ Shopping Bag

12-1/2" x 12" x 6"

Shop 'til you drop! -OR- Make a cute Diaper Bag! -OR- Make a great Beach Bag! It all depends upon which fabric you choose.

⌘ Supply List:

Basic Supplies
Timtex™: 1-3/4 yards
24" Steam-A-Seam 2® (S-A-S 2): 3-1/2 yards
Fabric 1 (exterior): 3/4 yard
Fabric 2 (interior): 1-1/8 yards
Buttons: (2) 1-1/8" cover buttons
Leather Strap: 1-1/2" x 40"
D-Ring: (1) for key clip
Fabric Glue: your favorite
    liquid fabric adhesive.
Thread to coordinate or contrast
Hook and Loop Tape 3/4": 4" (optional*)
    *Hook and Loop tape is used only if you
    are making the glasses case and/or the
    cell phone holder.

✂ Step 1. Cutting (see page 18)

Stack the pieces as you cut them. Each stack should contain (1) piece of Timtex™, (2) pieces of S-A-S 2 and (2) pieces of fabric. All pieces within the stack should have the same dimensions. Make a template (see page 16) from template plastic and mark it with the pattern letter for the Flaps, pattern piece L on page 40. Cut the Timtex™ as shown in Diagram 1.

Cut the S-A-S 2 as shown in Diagram 2.

Cut Fabric 1 and Fabric 2 as in Charts 1 & 2.

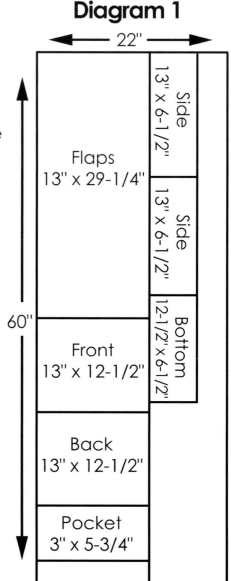

Diagram 1

← 22" →

Flaps
13" x 29-1/4"

Side
13" x 6-1/2"

Side
13" x 6-1/2"

Bottom
12-1/2" x 6-1/2"

60"

Front
13" x 12-1/2"

Back
13" x 12-1/2"

Pocket
3" x 5-3/4"

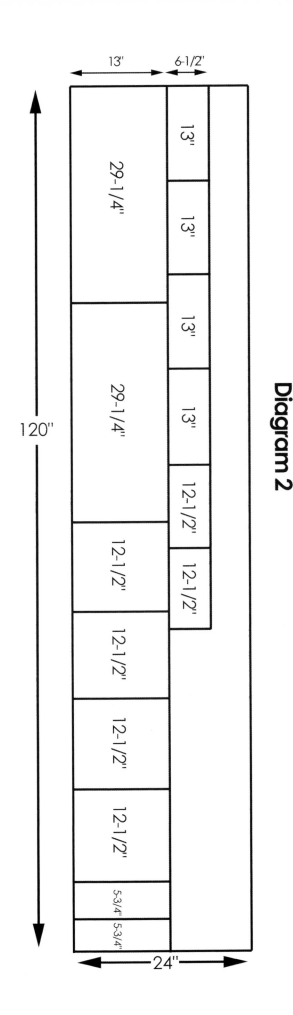

Diagram 2

Chart 1

Item	#	Size
Fabric 1	2	13" x 45"
Fabric 2	3	13" x 45"

Chart 2

Item	#	Size
Fabric 1		
Front & Back	2	13" x 12-1/2"
Sides	2	13" x 6-1/2"
Bottom	1	12-1/2" x 6-1/2"
Pocket	1	13" x 5-3/4"
Fabric 2		
Flaps	2	13" x 29-1/4"
Front & Back	2	13" x 12-1/2"
Sides	2	13" x 6-1/2"
Bottom	1	12-1/2" x 6-1/2"
Pocket	1	13" x 5-3/4"

⌘ Step 2. Sandwiching
(see page 20)

The Front and Back pieces will require special attention. One will need loop tape and the other will require the pocket sewn in place before fusing the exterior fabric to the sandwich. If you choose not to use the loop tape or the pocket, sandwich those pieces in the same manner as the Sides and Bottom. Otherwise set the Front and Back pieces aside and sandwich the remaining pieces. Each piece of Timtex™ will have S-A-S 2 and Fabric 1 on one side and S-A-S 2 and Fabric 2 on the other side. The exception to this concerns the Flaps, which require S-A-S 2 and Fabric 2 on both sides of the Timtex™. Be sure to steam iron each side of the sandwich until the fusing process is complete.

✂ Step 3. Recutting

Trim all the pieces down to the following sizes. *Again if you are making the pocket and using the hook and loop tape you will not have the Front and Back pieces in this step.

Chart 3

Item	#	Size
Front & Back*	2	12-1/2" x 12"
Sides	2	12-1/2" x 6"
Bottom	1	12" x 6"
Pocket	1	11-1/2" x 5-3/8"
Flaps	2	L
Flaps	2	L-R

⌘ Step 4. Preparing the Pocket

This pocket is designed to hold fairly flat objects such as a checkbook, a small pad or a shopping list. Satin stitch (see page 22) completely around the pocket piece and set it aside.

⌘ Step 5. Preparing the Front and Back

- Layer the Timtex with S-A-S 2 and the interior fabric (Fabric 2). Steam iron until the fusing process is complete. Trim the pieces down to 12-1/2" x 12".

- The loop tape can be attached in any location you choose. The bag on the cover has the tape attached at 2" down from the top and 2" in from each side. Cut the loop side of the tape in half making (2) 2" strips. Straight stitch the loop tape in place. It is important to back stitch at the beginning and end of the stitching. I also stitch around the tape twice.

- Place the prepared pocket piece 1/4" up from the bottom and centered on the second 12-1/2" x 12" piece. Straight stitch it in place. Start at the top of one side, pivot and sew along the bottom and then pivot and sew up the other side. Repeat this seam for greater stability and back stitch at the beginning and end of the seams. Divide the pocket according to the desired use. It is not advisable to divide it into more than 3 sections as it does not have a great deal of give.

- Sandwich the other side of these pieces with S-A-S 2 and Fabric 1 (exterior fabric). Trim down the fabric to the previously cut 12-1/2" x 12" sandwich.

⌘ Step 4. Satin Stitch
(see page 22)

- Satin stitch the sides and top of the Front and Back pieces.-
- Satin stitch these to the Bottom piece along the 12" side. This is only a joining seam so centering the seam between the two pieces is important and you need only stitch once at this time. Set this unit aside for now.
- Satin stitch the Flaps to the Sides. Line the tops of the Flaps and Side pieces up perfectly as this will provide for a smoothly finished bag top. If you are satin stitching twice, now is the time to do so on these seams. Satin stitch around the entire edge of these newly formed units except for the 6" bottom of the Side pieces. The drawing shows you what your units should look like (see drawing).
- Satin stitch these units to the Bottom piece.
- With the exterior fabric facing up, satin stitch around the entire bottom. Roll the large pieces before fitting them through the machine opening. This will not hurt the project as it can be ironed after the stitching is finished.

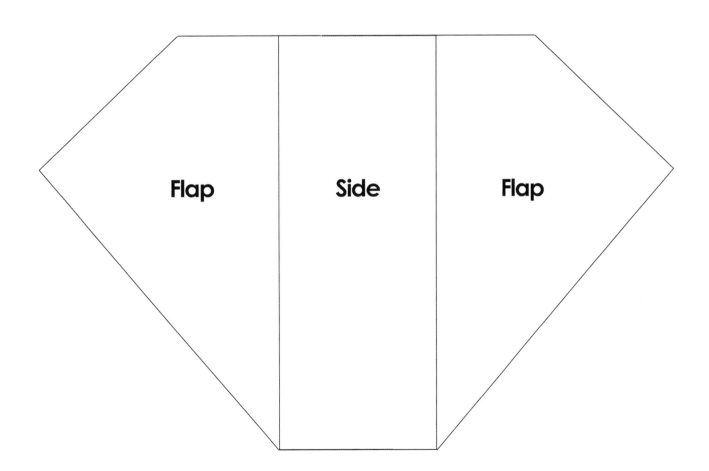

Flap　　　**Side**　　　**Flap**

⌘ Lunch Bag or Great Gift Bag

8-1/2" x 8" x 4"

Don't brown bag it ever again - not when you can *style* bag it with this fun bag.
-OR - Make a special gift bag and give it as a delightful part of the gift.

⌘ Supply List:

Basic Supplies
Timtex™: 5/8 yard
18" Steam-A-Seam 2® (S-A-S 2): 1-1/4 yard
Fabric 1 (exterior): 3/8 yard
Fabric 2 (interior): 3/8 yard
Thread to coordinate or contrast
Fabric Glue: your favorite liquid fabric adhesive
Handles: 1 set with horseshoe hooks
Buttons: 2

✂ Step 1. Cutting (see page 18)

Stack the pieces as you cut them. Each stack should contain (1) piece of Timtex™, (2) pieces of fabric and (2) pieces of S-A-S 2. All pieces within each stack should have the same dimensions. Make a template (see page 16) for the flaps, (pattern piece H) (page 49) from template plastic and mark it with the pattern letter.

Chart 1

Item	#	Size
Timtex™	2	8-3/4" x 22"
	1	4-1/4" x 22"
Fabric 1	1	13" x 45"
Fabric 2	1	13" x 45"
18" S-A-S 2	1	13" x 18"
	2	8-1/4" x 18"
	2	4-1/4" x 18"
	1	4-1/4" x 18"
	1	1" x 18"

Chart 2

Item	#	Size
Timtex™		
Front & Back	2	8-3/4" x 8-1/4"
Bottom	1	4-1/4" x 8-1/4"
Sides	2	4-1/4" x 8-3/4"
Tabs	2	4-1/4" x 1"
Flaps	1	8-3/4" x 13"
Fabric 1		
Flaps	1	13" x 8-3/4"
Front & Back	2	8-3/4" x 8-1/4"
Sides	2	8-3/4" x 4-1/4"
Bottom	1	8-1/4" x 4-1/4"
Tabs	2	4-1/4" x 1"
Fabric 2		
Flaps	1	13" x 8-3/4"
Front & Back	2	8-3/4" x 8-1/4"
Sides	2	8-3/4" x 4-1/4"
Bottom	1	8-1/4" x 4-1/4"
Tabs	2	4-1/4" x 1"
S-A-S 2		
Flaps	2	13" x 8-3/4"
Front & Back	4	8-3/4" x 8-1/4"
Sides	4	8-3/4" x 4-1/4"
Bottom	2	8-1/4" x 4-1/4"
Tabs	4	4-1/4" x 1"

⌘ Step 2. Sandwiching
(see page 20)

Each piece of Timtex™ needs S-A-S 2, and fabric on each side. All pieces will have Fabric 1 on one side and Fabric 2 on the other side. Be sure to steam iron each side of the sandwich until the fusing process is complete.

✂ Step 3. Recutting

Trim down the sandwich pieces to the sizes in Chart 3.

Chart 3

Item	#	Size
Bottom	1	8" x 4"
Sides	2	8-1/2" x 4"
Front & Back	2	8-1/2" x 8"
Tabs	2	3/4" x 4-1/4"
Flaps	2	H
Flaps	2	H-R

⌘ Step 4. Satin Stitch
(see page 22)

- Satin stitch the sides and top of each of the Side pieces.
- Satin stitch these to the Bottom piece. (The normal exterior fabric is the interior fabric for the Bottom only.) Stitch only one time to hold the Side pieces in place for now. Set the unit aside.
- Satin stitch Flaps to the Front and Back. (see drawing) Fabric 2 is the exterior of the Flaps.

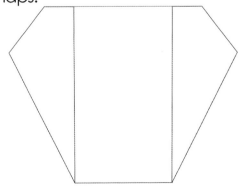

- Satin stitch all the way around the newly formed front and back units, except the bottom section of the Front and Back pieces

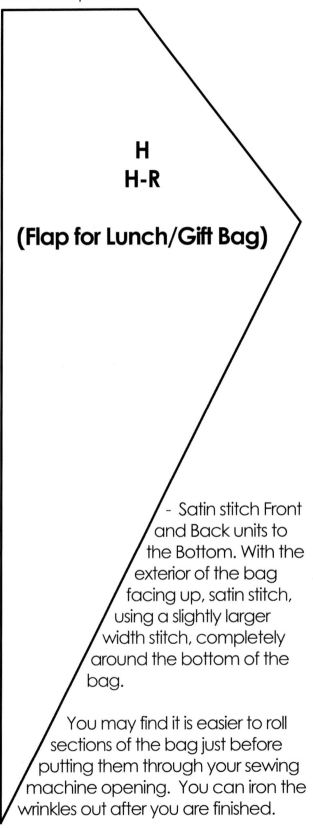

H
H-R
(Flap for Lunch/Gift Bag)

- Satin stitch Front and Back units to the Bottom. With the exterior of the bag facing up, satin stitch, using a slightly larger width stitch, completely around the bottom of the bag.

You may find it is easier to roll sections of the bag just before putting them through your sewing machine opening. You can iron the wrinkles out after you are finished.

⌘ Step 5. Tabs

NOW IS THE TIME TO DECIDE WHAT HANDLES YOU WANT TO USE.

If you decide to use handles that are on one of the other bags, you need to look at the Handles and Hardware section (see page 84) and make the needed adjustments.

To make the bag as it is shown, continue on with these instructions.

- Satin stitch the long sides of the Tab sandwich pieces. (0.3mm length and 4.0mm width)

- Cut (4) 1-1/2" pieces from the 3/4" wide strips. Carefully fold the Tabs in half and iron in a permanent crease. Be sure the ends are perfectly even. Handles are not always exactly the same width apart so be sure to measure the width of each handle. Center the handle width on the Front and Back of the bag and mark those spots. You will need to sew the Tabs on at these markings. Center the Tabs over the marks and place them 3/8" below the edge of the bag top. If you want to straight stitch the Tabs into place first be sure to stitch as close to the edge of the Tabs as possible. Satin stitch Tabs in place. (0.3mm length and 4.0 width)

⌘ Step 6. Cross-Over Construction A (see page24)

Follow the instructions for construction A.

⌘ Step 7. Embelishment
(see page 91)

Follow the instructions on how to attach the buttons on the bags.

⌘ Step 8. Handles (see page 89)

Follow the instructions on how to attach the handles with horseshoe hooks.

⌘ Photo Gallery

Evening
Take-Out
Bag

Music Bag

Shopping Bag

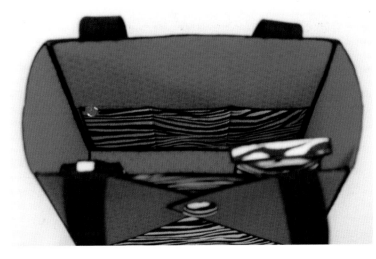

Lunch or Great Gift Bag

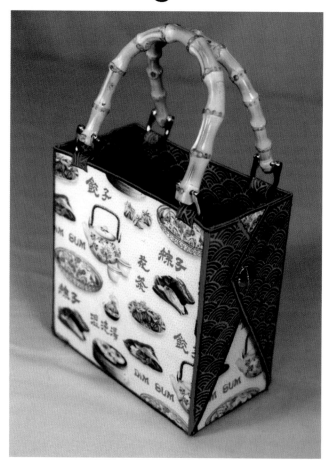

Hand
Bag

Checkin' In

Credit Card Holder

Glasses Case

Cell
Phone
Holder

Cozy Coasters

⌘ Cross-Over Hand Bag

10-1/2" x 10" x 5"

I have never carried this bag without someone stopping me and asking where I got it! It's so much fun and has a great little zippered pocket that is just right for your money and credit cards.

⌘ Supply List:

Timtex™: 1-1/4 yard
12" Steam-A- Seam 2® (S-A-S 2): 3-5/8 yard
Fabric 1 (exterior): 5/8 yard *
Fabric 2 (interior): 1/3 yard
Fabric 3 (flaps): 2/3 yard
Thread to coordinate or contrast
Zipper: 9 inch, (dress-weight nylon)
Fabric Glue: your favorite liqud fabric adhesive
Tassel: (1)
Magnetic Snap: 1 set
Buttons: (1) 7/8" and (2) 1-1/8" Cover Buttons
Zipper Foot
Handles and Attachments: 1 set (2 handles and 4 horseshoe hooks)
   *If Fabric 3 is used to make the inside zippered pocket,
     only 1/3 yard of Fabric 1 is needed.

✂ Step 1. Cutting (see page 18)

Stack the pieces as you cut them. With the exception of the pocket pieces, each stack should contain (1) piece of Timtex™, (2) pieces of fabric and (2) pieces of S-A-S 2. All pieces within the stack should have the same dimensions. Make a template for pieces I, J and K from template plastic and mark them with the pattern letter (see page 16). Be sure to transfer the markings to your templates. Cut the pieces found in Chart 1 first, and from those cut the pieces in Chart 2.

Chart 1

Item	#	Size
Timtex™	1	10-1/2" x 22"
	1	5-1/2" x 22"
	1	28" x 22"
S-A-S 2	4	12" x 10-1/2"
	6	12" x 5-1/2"
	1	12" x 56"
Fabric 1	1	11" x 42"
*	*1	*8-1/2" x 42"
Fabric 2	1	11" x 42"
Fabric 3	2	11" x 42"

*Do not cut pocket pieces from Fabric 1 if you have purchased only 1/3 yard. Cut pocket pieces from only one of the fabrics. (Fabric 1 - OR- Fabric 3)

Chart 2

Item	#	Size
Timtex™		
Front & Back	2	10-1/2" x 11"
Sides (I)	2	5-1/2" x 11"
Flaps (J)	1	11" x 28"
Bottom	1	10-1/2" x 5-1/2"
Handle Tabs	1	1" x 7"
Closure Tab (K)	1	2" x 5"
S-A-S 2		
Front & Back	4	11" x 10-1/2"
Sides (I)	4	11" x 5-1/2"
Flaps (J)	2	11" x 28"
Bottom	2	10-1/2" x 5-1/2"
Handle Tabs	2	1" x 7"
Closure Tab (K)**	2	2" x 5"
Fabric 1		
Front & Back	2	10-1/2" x 11"
Sides (I)	2	5-1/2" x 11"
*Pocket	1	8-1/2" x 7"
*Pocket	1	5-1/2" x 7"
Handle Tabs	2	1" x 7"
Fabric 2		
Front & Back	2	10-1/2" x 11"
Sides (I)	2	5-1/2" x 11"
Fabric 3		
Flaps (J)	2	11" x 28"
Bottom	2	10-1/2" x 5-1/2"
*Pocket	1	8-1/2" x 7"
*Pocket	1	5-1/2" x 7"
Closure Tab (K)	2	2" x 5"

** This piece of S-A-S 2 will need to be pieced. Instructions on how to piece S-A-S 2 are in the general instructions under fusible web (see page 12).

⌘ Step 2. Preparing the Pocket

This pocket is easy to make!

a) Place the two pieces of pocket fabric right sides together. Line up the 7" portion on one of the ends and baste it together with a 3/4" seam. Press the seam open. With the wrong side of the fabric facing up, place the zipper face down on the seam. The zipper pull should be completely past the end of the fabric with the tab extended. Center the zipper along the seam line. Using a zipper foot, straight stitch along each side of the zipper. Without pulling the basting seam out, gently open the zipper past the fabric edge about 2". Be sure the zipper pull is well inside the body of the pocket. An easy way to open the zipper at this point is to use a ballpoint pen that can be closed. Close it and put the closed end in the hole of the zipper pull and push it open.
(see drawing below)

b) Straight stitch across the ends of the zipper. Cut off the portion of the zipper that extends past the sides of the pocket. (see drawing below)

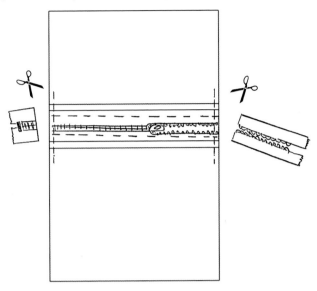

c) Fold the pocket in half with the right sides together. Carefully line up the sides and the 7" ends of the pocket. With a 1/2" seam allowance, straight stitch down one side, across the bottom and up the other side. Back stitch at both ends. (see drawing below)

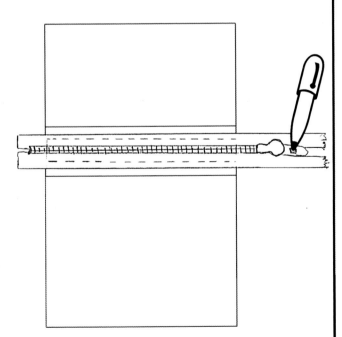

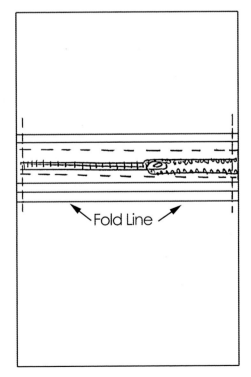

Fold Line

d) Open the zipper and pull the basting seam out. Cut diagonally across the corners and turn the pocket right side out (see drawing below). Press the pocket flat.

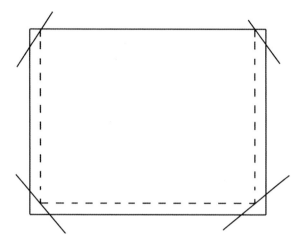

e) The zipper will be much easier to use if you attach a zipper pull. A small tassel slipped through the hole and back through its own loop makes a classy decorative touch.

⌘ Step 3. Installing the Pocket

You will be using the stack of Timtex™, S-A-S 2 and fabric needed for the Back. Layer S-A-S 2, Timtex™ and the interior fabric for the back. Steam iron until the fusing process is complete. Place the pocket at the desired spot and straight stitch it into place stitching completely around the pocket. Be sure to back stitch at the beginning and end of your stitching. I usually center the pocket and place it 2" down from the top of the Back piece. The nice thing about this pattern is having a lot of freedom to make those decisions according to your needs. Now layer the other side of the Back piece with the remaining S-A-S 2, and the exterior fabric. Steam

iron until the fusing process is complete. Set this unit aside and trim it down with the rest of the pieces.

⌘ Step 4. Installing the Magnetic Clasp

The stack of Timtex™, S-A-S 2 and fabric needed for the Front piece is used for this step. Layer the Timtex™, S-A-S 2 and the exterior fabric and steam iron this side until the fusing process is complete. Trim the piece down to 10-1/2" x 10". On the fabric side of this piece, find the center of the top and measure 3/4" down. This is where one side of the magnetic clasp will be placed. Refer to Handles and Hardware (see page 84) and follow the instructions for installing the magnetic clasp. Layer the other

side with the remaining S-A-S 2 and the interior fabric for the Front piece. Steam iron until the fusing process is complete. Set this unit aside and trim it down with the rest of the pieces.

⌘ Step 5. Sandwiching
(see page 20)

Each piece of Timtex™ needs S-A-S 2 and fabric on each side. The Front, Back and Sides should have Fabric 1 on one side and Fabric 2 on the other side. The Handle Tabs should have Fabric 1 on both sides. The Flaps (J), Bottom and Closure Tab (K) should have Fabric 3 on both sides. Layer the stacks and steam iron each side until the fusing process is complete.

⌘ Step 6. Recutting

Trim down the pieces to the sizes in Chart 3.

Chart 3

Item	#	Size
Front and Back	2	10-1/2" x 10"
*Sides (I)	2	10-1/2" x 5"
Flaps (J)	4	J
Bottom	1	10" x 5"
Handle Tabs	1	3/4" x 7"
**Closure Tab (K)	1	K

*Do not cut the seam lines on the Sides (I) at this time.
**The Closure Tab is long. You may want to cut it shorter but at this time it is advisable to cut it the length of the template. It can be cut down later when the desired length is determined.

⌘ Step 7. Preparing the Sides

The Sides on this bag have a seam that allows the Closure Tab to pull the top of the bag closed. Transfer the cutting lines to the outside of the 10-1/2" x 5" Side (I) pieces. Cut along the cutting lines. Be sure the pieces don't get mixed up. Satin stitch the pieces back together along the same lines. If you are satin stitching your seams twice, now is the time to do so on these seams.

⌘ Step 8. Satin Stitch (see page 22)

- Satin stitch the sides and top of the Front and Back pieces.

- Satin stitch the Front and Back pieces to the 10" side of the Bottom piece.

- Satin stitch the Flaps (J) to the Side (I) pieces (see drawing). Stitch these seams twice at this time.

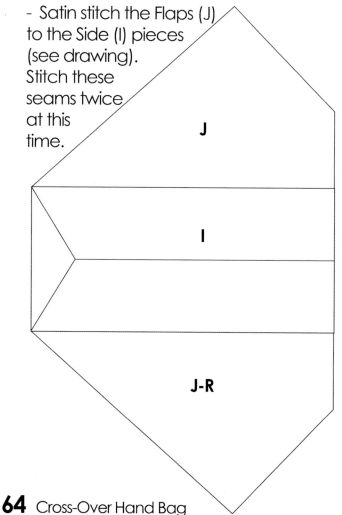

- Satin stitch all the way around the exterior of this unit except for the bottom section of the Side pieces.

- Satin stitch the Side/Flap units to the Bottom piece along the 5" edge (see drawing).

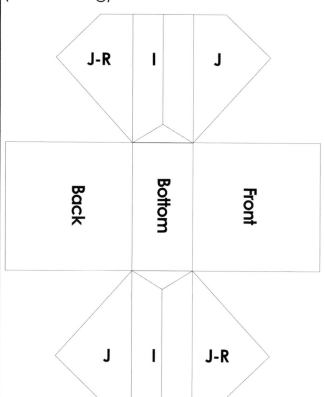

- With the exterior of the bag facing up, satin stitch completely around the bottom of the bag. Be sure to use a bit wider stitch to cover the stitching used to connect the pieces. You may find it is easier to roll sections of the bag just before putting them through your sewing machine opening. The wrinkles can be ironed out after you are finished. Set this unit aside.

⌘ Step 9. Preparing the Closure Tab

- Satin stitch around the sides and pointed end of the Closure Tab in one continuous seam.

- Determine the desired length for the Closure Tab. The full length of the tab will leave the bag open by approximately 2". Cutting it down to the solid cutting line, will close the opening to approximately 1-1/4".

- Refer to Handles and Hardware (see page 84) to install the magnetic clasp on the pointed end of the Closure Tab. The placement for the magnetic clasp is at the center of the tab and 1/2" from the tip.

- Satin stitch the flat edge of the Closure Tab to the outside of the Back piece. The washer side of the Closure Tab should be facing up. Center it 3/4" down from the top edge of the Back piece. Be sure this will line up properly with the clasp which has already been inserted on the Front piece. To further secure the Closure Tab a second row of satin stitching can be sewn across the top of the bag over the Closure Tab.

⌘ Step 10. Handle Tab Insertion

NOW IS THE TIME TO DECIDE WHAT HANDLES YOU DESIRE TO USE.
If you decide to use handles from one of the other bags, reference the Handles and Hardware section (see page 84) and make the needed adjustments.

To make the bag as it is shown, continue on with these instructions.

- Satin stitch the long sides of the Handle Tab sandwich pieces. (0.3mm length and 4.0mm width)

- Cut (4) 1-1/2" pieces from the 3/4" wide strips. Carefully fold the Tabs in half and iron in a permanent crease. Be sure the ends are perfectly even. Handles are not always exactly the same width apart so be sure to measure the width of each handle. Center the handle width on the Front and Back of the bag and mark those spots. The Handle Tabs will be attached at these markings. Center the Tabs over the marks and place them 3/8" below the edge of the bag top. If you want to straight stitch the Tabs into place first, be sure to stitch as close to the edge of the Tabs as possible. Satin stitch the Tabs in place. (0.3mm length and 4.0 width)

⌘ Step 11. Tacking the Sides

Fold the Side piece in half along the center seam. The exterior fabric will be touching. Satin stitch about 1/4" at the top of the fold, as close to the center seam as you can. Don't forget to lock stitch at the beginning and the end of the satin stitch tack.

⌘ Step 12. Cross-Over Construction B (see page 24)
Follow the instructions for Construction B.

⌘ Step 13. Embelishment (see page 91)

Follow the instructions on how to cover buttons and how to attach them to the bag.

⌘ Step 14. Handles (see page 84)
Follow the instructions on how to attach the handles with horseshoe hooks.

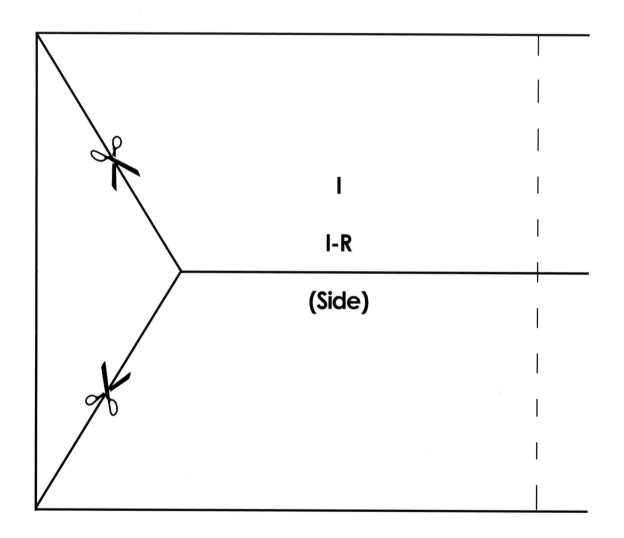

I

I-R

(Side)

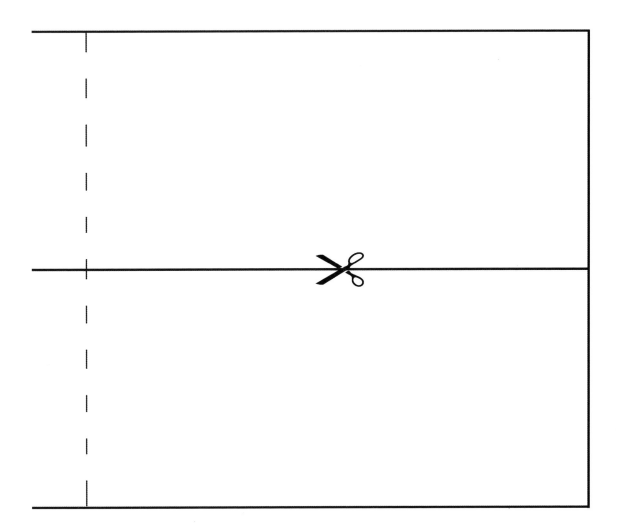

-Photocopy both pages.

-Tape them together at the dotted line before making your template. Be sure to label the template with the appropriate letters.

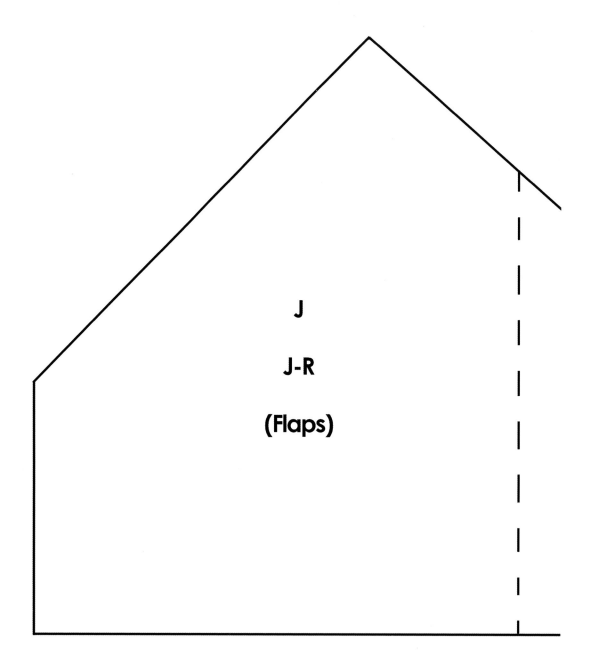

J

J-R

(Flaps)

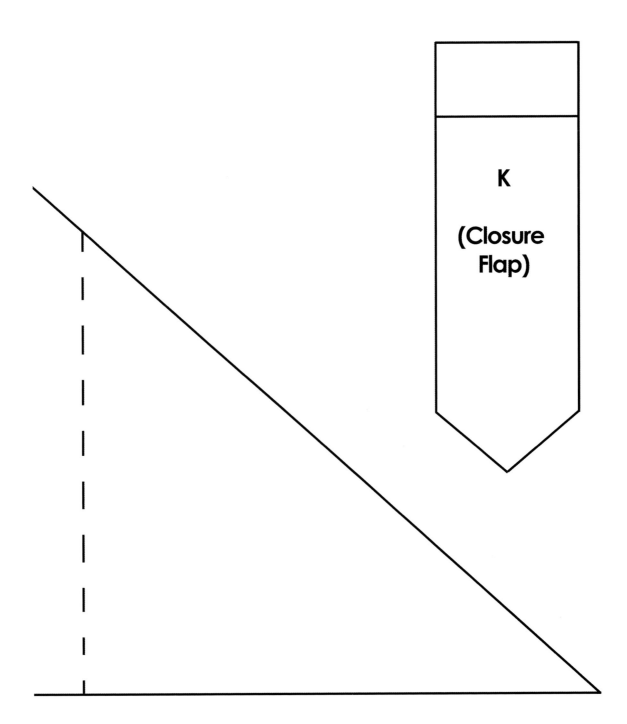

-Photocopy both pages.

-Tape them together at the dotted line before making your template. Be sure to label the template with the appropriate letters.

⌘ Credit Card/Calculator/ Business Card Holder

4" x 3"

This little gem is great for carrying your credit cards, business cards and even a little calculator. I load it with just the necessities for a trip to a bazaar or event where I need a number of business cards, a calculator, and just one credit card! This card holder is always a hit when made from the same fabric as my handbag.

⌘ Supply List:

Basic supplies
Timtex™: 1/8 yard
12" Steam-A-Seam 2® (S-A-S 2): 1/4 yard
Fabric 1: 1/8 yard
Fabric 2: 1/8 yard
Vinyl, 16 gauge clear or 12 gauge frosted*: 1/8 yard (4-1/2" x 15")
Thread to coordinate or contrast
Waxed paper
Nickel (1)
   *Frosted vinyl is not as sticky and may be the better choice.

✂ Step 1. Cutting (see page 18)

Item	#	Size
Timtex™	1	6-1/4" x 4-1/4"
S-A-S 2	2	6-1/4" x 4-1/4"
Fabric 1	1	6-1/4" x 4-1/4"
Fabric 2	1	6-1/4" x 4-1/4"
Vinyl	2	4" x 2-1/2"
Vinyl	2	4-1/4" x 5"

⌘ Step 2. Sandwiching
(see page 20)

Layer the 6-1/4" x 4-1/4" pieces of Timtex™, S-A-S 2, Fabric 1 and Fabric 2. Steam iron each side until the fusing process is complete.

✂ Step 3. Recutting

Trim down the sandwich to 6" x 4" and round the corners using the nickel to mark them before trimming. Cut the sandwich in half, making (2) 3" x 4" pieces. Satin stitch them back together along that seam (see page 22). This will allow for a better fold. It can be difficult to see the center of this seam so you may want to mark it before cutting to aid you in centering your satin stitched seam. Satin stitch all around the outer edge and don't forget to lock stitch (see page 23).

⌘ Step 4. Preparing the Vinyl

Round both corners on one 4" side of each of the 4" x 2-1/2" pieces of vinyl. They should now match the corners of the outer cover. On one piece of the 4-1/4" x 5" vinyl cut a half circle in the center of the 4-1/4" ends using a nickel as a template. Mark a line using a ballpoint pen down the center of this piece dividing the 5 inches in half (see drawing). Lay this piece on top of the other 4-1/4" x 5" piece of vinyl. Line up all the sides evenly. Straight stitch a 1/4" seam along the 5" sides. Use waxed paper on the top and underside of the vinyl. Be sure to backstitch all seam ends. Remove paper carefully and trim seams down to 1/8". Set aside.

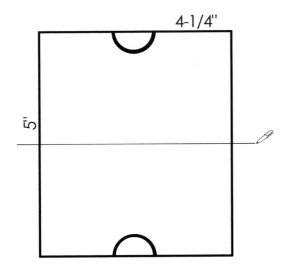

4-1/4"

5"

⌘ Step 5. Assembling

Lay the cover open with the outside facing up. Place a 4" x 2-1/2" piece of vinyl over one end carefully lining up the rounded corners. Place waxed paper over the vinyl and straight stitch in the ditch (see page 23) of the satin stitch from one side around the bottom and up the other side. Be sure to backstitch at the beginning and the end of the seams. Leave the 4" straight side of the vinyl open. Repeat this on the other end of the cover.

⌘ Step 6. Inserting the Vinyl Sleeve

Lay the cover open with the inside up. Carefully center the inked line on the 4-1/4" x 5" piece of vinyl over the center satin stitched seam of the cover. Place waxed paper under the cover and on top of the vinyl insert and straight stitch down the inked center line. Be sure you remember to back stitch at the beginning and the end of each seam. Carefully remove the waxed paper. Fold the case in half and Voila, you have your case.

⌘ **Checkin' In** (Checkbook Cover)

6-1/2" x 3-5/8"

Now you can individualize your checkbook cover to go with any of the bags you create or just make some fun covers as gifts.

⌘ **Supply List:**

Basic Supplies
Timtex™: 1/4 yard.
12" Steam-A-Steam 2® (S-A-S 2): 2/3 yard
Fabric 1 (exterior and pocket): 1/4 yard
Fabric 2 (interior): 1/4 yard
Thread to coordinate or contrast
Vinyl, 16 gauge clear or 12 gauge frosted*: 6" x 2-7/8"
Waxed paper
   *Frosted vinyl is not as sticky and may be the better choice.

✂ Step 1. Cutting (see page 18)

Item	#	Size
Timtex™	1	7" x 7-3/4"
S-A-S 2	2	7" x 7-3/4"
	2	6-1/2" x 3"
Fabric 1	1	7" x 7-3/4"
	2	6-1/2" x 6"
Fabric 2	1	7" x 7-3/4"
Vinyl	1	6-1/4" x 2-7/8"

⌘ Step 2. Sandwiching
(see page 20)

Layer the 7-3/4" x 7" pieces of Timtex™, S-A-S 2, Fabric 1 and Fabric 2 then steam iron each side until the fusing process is complete.

✂ Step 3. Recutting

Trim the sandwich down to 6-1/2" x 7-1/4". Cut it in half making (2) 6-1/2" x 3-5/8" pieces. Satin stitch (0.3mm length, 6.0mm width see page 22) these pieces back together. This will allow for a better fold. It can be difficult to see the center of this seam. You may want to mark it before cutting to aid you in centering your satin stitch.

⌘ Step 4. Preparation of Pockets

You will make two pockets. For each pocket, place a 6-1/2" x 3" piece of S-A-S 2 on the wrong side of a 6-1/2" x 6" piece of Fabric 1 carefully lining up the 6-1/2" sides. Fold crisply along the center edge of the S-A-S 2 and steam iron until the fusing process is complete. Satin stitch (0.3mm length, 4.0mm width) along the folded edge of each pocket.

⌘ Step 5. Assembling

With satin stitched pocket edge facing the satin stitched center seam of the inside of the cover, line the raw edge of the pocket up with the top of the cover. Do the same with the bottom pocket. Baste the pockets in place as close to the edge as possible. Satin stitch completely around the outer edge (0.3mm length, 6.0mm width, see page 22). Don't forget to lock stitch at both ends.

⌘ Step 6. Adding the Vinyl Carbon Guard

If you don't have carbon checks, you won't need to follow this step. You're finished! However, if you do need the carbon check guard, cut a piece of vinyl to 6" x 2-7/8". Center it along the bottom edge of the bottom pocket. Cover it with waxed paper before straight stitching in the ditch (see page 23) of the satin stitched edge of the cover. Be sure to back stitch on both ends of the seam. Gently remove the waxed paper.

⌘ Glasses Case

4" x 7"

Whether you wear glasses or sunglasses you will have a favorite place to put them after you make this easy project.

⌘ Supply List:

Basic Supplies
Timtex™: 1/8 yard
12" Steam-A-Seam 2: 3/8 yard
Fabric 1 (exterior): 1/4 yard
Fabric 2 (interior): 1/4 yard
Thread to coordinate or contrast
Hook and Loop Tape: *optional 2"
   *Hook and loop tape is used
   only if you are making the
   shopping bag with all the
   extras or if you want to glue
   one side of the tape to a
   dashboard or some other
   special place you may want
   easy access to your glasses.

Chart 1

Item	#	Size
Timtex™	1	4-1/4" x 7-1/4"
	1	4-1/4" x 1"
	1	4-1/4" x 5-3/4"
	1	4-1/4" x 2-3/4"
12" S-A-S 2	2	4-1/4" x 7-1/4"
	2	4-1/4" x 1"
	2	4-1/4" x 5-3/4"
	2	4-1/4" x 2-3/4"
Fabric 1	1	4-1/4" x 7-1/4"
	1	4-1/4" x 1"
	1	4-1/4" x 5-3/4"
	1	4-1/4" x 2-3/4" (M)
Fabric 2	1	4-1/4" x 7-1/4"
	1	4-1/4" x 1"
	1	4-1/4" x 5-3/4"
	1	4-1/4" x 2-3/4"
	1	7-1/2" x 1-1/4"

✂ Step 1. Cutting (see page 18)

Stack pieces as you cut them. Each stack should contain (1) piece of Timtex™, (2) pieces of fabric and (2) pieces of S-A-S 2. All pieces within the stack should have the same dimensions. Make the template (see page 16) for the Case Flap (M on page 75) from template plastic and mark it with the pattern letter. Trim the full length of Timtex™ down to 4-1/4" x 22".

⌘ Step 2. Sandwiching
(see page 20)

If you intend to use the hook and loop tape on this project, first you will need to sandwich the 4-1/4" x 7-1/4" pieces using the exterior fabric, one piece of S-A-S 2 and the Timtex™. Now trim it down to 4" x 7". Straight stitch the hook side of the tape to the fabric side of this piece, center it 1-1/2" down from the top. Save the loop side to use in the shopping bag or to adhere to the desired surface. Finish sandwiching the second piece of S-A-S 2 and the interior fabric on the other side. If you do not intend to use the hook and loop tape, sandwich all the pieces. Be sure to steam iron until the fusing process is complete.

✂ Step 3. Recutting
Trim all pieces down to the following sizes.

Chart 2

From	To
4-1/4" x 1"	4" x 1"
4-1/4" x 5-3/4"	4" x 5-1/2"
4-1/4" x 2-3/4"	M
** 4-1/4" x 7-1/4"	**4" x 7"

** If you have used the hook and loop tape, this piece has already been trimmed. If not, then it needs to be trimmed at this time.

⌘ Step 4. Preparing the Fabric Latch Strip

Lay the 7-1/2" x 1-1/4" piece of fabric face down on the ironing board. Fold the fabric in and iron 1/4" on each side. Fold this piece in half matching the folded edges together and straight stitch both sides. Set this aside for the time being.

⌘ Step 5. Assembling
(see Satin Stitch page 22)

All Pieces should be joined with the exterior piece face up.
- Lay the 4" x 5-1/2" piece face up and measure 1/2" down from the top. Straight stitch the closure strip in place. Stitch as close to the edge as possible. This is only to hold it in place until you satin stitch the edges of the case together.
- Satin stitch the top of the 4" x 5-1/2" piece. Join this piece at the bottom end to the 4" x 7" piece with a satin stitch seam.
- Join the 4" x 1" piece to the 4" x 7" piece with a satin stitch seam.
- Join the closure flap to the 4" x 1" piece with a satin stitch seam.
- Fold the 4" x 5-1/2" front piece along the seam line. At this point, be sure the exterior fabric is on the exterior.
- Satin stitch all the way around the exterior of the case.
- Fold the seams on each side of the 4" X 1" piece and slip the angled cover into the latch strap.

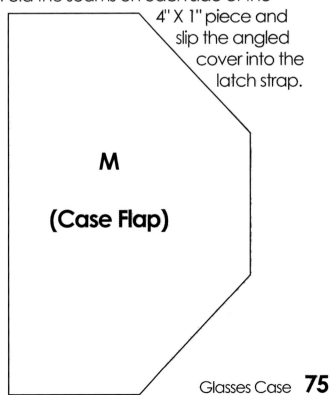

M

(Case Flap)

⌘ Cell Phone Holder

3-1/2" x 2-1/2" x 1"

Purchase a little extra hook and loop tape and adhere some of the loop side to any surface you may find a need for a *Cell Phone Holder*. It is designed for use in the *Shopping Bag*.

⌘ Supply List:

Timtex™: 1/8 yard
12" Steam-A-Seam 2 (S-A-S 2):
    1/2 yard
Fabric 1: 1/8 yard
Fabric 2: 1/8 yard
Thread to coordinate or
    contrast and a small amount
    of thread to coordinate with
    Fabric 1 for use in the bobbin
Hook and Loop Tape 3/4": 3"
Button: (1)
Fabric Glue: your favorite
    liquid fabric adhesive

✂ Step 1. Cutting (see page 18)

Cut pieces as indicated in Chart 1.

Item	#	Size
Timtex™	1	3-3/4" x 22"
12" S-A-S 2	4	3-3/4" x 12"
Fabric 1	1	3-3/4" x 45"
Fabric 2	1	3-3/4" x 45"

⌘ Step 2. Sandwiching
(see page 20)

All pieces will be cut from one sandwich. Make a template (see page 16) for pattern pieces N and P and set these aside. Layer S-A-S 2 and Fabric 1 on one side of the Timtex™ and S-A-S 2 and Fabric 2 on the other side. Cut off the excess fabric from both sides. Steam iron each side until the fusing process is complete.

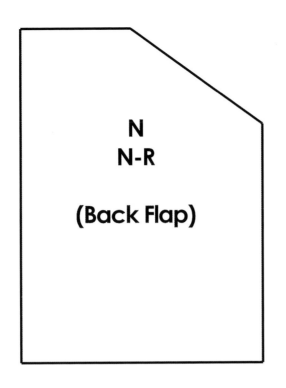

N
N-R

(Back Flap)

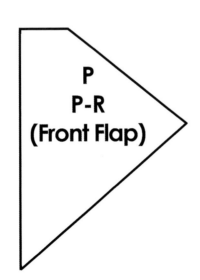

P
P-R
(Front Flap)

✂ Step 3. Recutting

- Square off an end of the sandwich strip and cut (1) 3/4" strip from that end. Trim this piece down to 3" x 3/4".

- Trim the entire strip down to 3-1/2" wide. Cut (3) 3-1/2" x 2-1/2" pieces from the strip. One (1) is the Back and (2) are for the Back Flaps (N, N-R). Cut one each of N and N-R.

- Trim the remaining strip down to 2-1/2" wide. Cut (1) Front piece 2-1/2" x 2-1/2" square.

- Cut (3) 1" x 2-1/2" strips. These are the (2) Side pieces and the Bottom piece.

- Cut (1) piece from template P and one piece from template P-R. These are the Front Flaps.

⌘ Step 4. Satin Stitch

- Cut (1) 1/2" set of hook and loop tape. Cut a 2" piece of the hook side of the tape.

- Use thread in the bobbin that coordinates with Fabric 1 for this straight stitching. Straight stitch the 1/2" of hook tape in place on the Fabric 2 side of the Closing Strap (3-1/4" x 3/4"). See the drawing for placement.

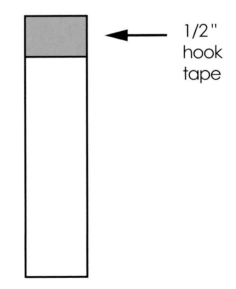

1/2"
hook
tape

- Straight stitch the 1/2" of loop tape at the top and centered on the Front piece (2-1/2" square) on the Fabric 1 side.

- Straight stitch the 2" hook side of the tape to the Fabric 2 side of one of the Back Flap pieces. Place it vertically, 1/4" down from the top and centered. The corner of the tape will touch the angled edge. See the drawing for placement.

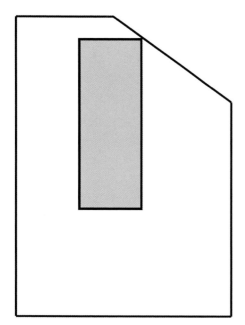

⌘ Step 4. Satin Stitch
(see page 22)

- Satin stitch a Back Flap and a Front Flap to a Side piece. Note which fabric needs to be facing up by looking at the drawing. If you are satin stitching your seams twice now is the time to do so on these seams.

- Satin stitch the sides and top of the Front piece and set it aside.

- Satin stitch (0.3mm length and 4.0mm width) the sides and hook end of the Closing Strap. This should be one continuous seam, and should be stitched twice. Leave the bottom unstitched.

- Satin stitch the unstitched end of the Closing Strap (0.4mm length and 4.0 mm width) to the top of Back piece by butting the two pieces together. The strap piece should be centered on the Back piece. Fabric 1 should be facing up on both pieces. Stitch only once at this time.

- Satin stitch the sides and top of the Back piece. This should be one continuous seam. Sewing over the connecting seam of the Back and Closing Strap will strengthen that seam.

- Satin stitch the Front and the Back pieces to the Bottom piece. Stitching once is sufficient at this time. Fabric 1 should be facing up on all pieces.

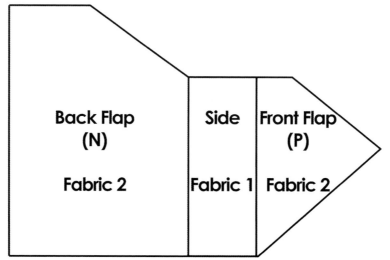

- Satin stitch completely around the Side/Flap units with the exception of the bottom of the Side pieces.

- Satin stitch the Side/Flap units to the Bottom (see drawing).

- With Fabric 1 facing up, satin stitch completely around the bottom.

⌘ Step 6. Cross-Over Construction B (see page 24)

Don't let the different shape of the Back Flaps confuse you. It is still the same construction. It is best to stitch the Front Flaps in place first using the stitch in the ditch technique (see page 23). It really doesn't matter which Front Flap crosses over first. I choose the best looking one for the outside. When crossing over the Back Flaps be sure to stitch the flap in place first that does not have the hook tape attached to it.

⌘ Step 7. Embellishments (see page 91)

An attractive button or some beads sewn at the Cross-Over point is a great way to finish up the Cell Phone Holder.

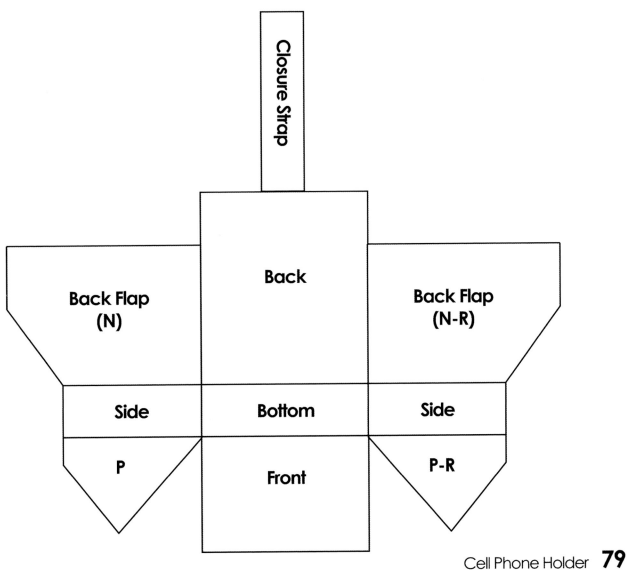

⌘ Cozy Coasters

Coasters 4" x 4"   Box 3" x 4-1/8" x 1-1/4"

I enjoy giving unique gifts. Try snagging a little fabric from a friend's redecorating project. Create this fun set of 10 coasters nestled in a little matching box and sneak them back into the newly decorated room. It's great sport!

⌘ Supply List:

Basic supplies
Timtex™: 1/2 yard
24"Steam-A-Seam 2® (S-A-S 2): 3/4 yd
      -OR-
12"Steam-A-Seam 2® (S-A-S 2): 1-1/2 yd

	Pink and Blue	
Fabric 1	1/8 yard (blue)	
Fabric 2	1/4 yard (pink)	
Fabric 3	1/8 yard (multi)	

	Blue and Butterfly	
Fabric 1	1/8 yard (blue)	
Fabric 2	1/4 yard (butterfly)	
Fabric 3	1/8 yard (yellow)	

-OR-

	Animal Print	
Fabric 1	1/8 yard (small leopard print)	
Fabric 2	1/8 yard (large leopard print)	
Fabric 3	1/8 yard (tiger print)	
Fabric 4	1/8 yard (black)	

(True solids are not recommended for the coasters as they will show water spots easily.)

Fabric Glue: your favorite liquid fabric adhesive
Beads to your liking
Small Hand Needle: One that has a small enough eye
   to pass through the beads of your choice.
Thread to coordinate or contrast with your fabrics
Fabric Marker: (It needs to be removable without washing.)

Coasters

✂ Step 1. Cutting (see page 18)

Item	#	Size
Timtex™	2	4-1/4" x 22"
24" S-A-S 2	4	4-1/4" x 24"
-OR-		
12" S-A-S 2	8	4-1/4" x 12"
Fabric 1	1	4-1/4" x 45"
Fabric 2	1	4-1/4" x 45"

✂ Step 2. Recutting Fabrics and Sandwiching

Cut fabrics in half making (2) 4-1/4" x approximately 22" pieces of each fabric. Sandwich (see page 20), layer the pieces of Timtex™, S-A-S 2, Fabric 1 and Fabric 2, and then steam iron each side until the fusing process is complete.

✂ Step 3. Recutting

Trim the sandwich down to 4" strips, square off the end and cut (5) 4" squares from each strip. You should have a total of 10 squares.

⌘ Step 4. Satin Stitch

Satin stitch (see page 22) around all 4 sides of each coaster; lock stitch.
Set them aside and start on the box.

Box

✂ Step 1. Cutting (see page 18)

Make the template (see page 16) for the Flaps, pattern piece (G) from template plastic and mark it with pattern letter. Stack the pieces, as you cut them with the template, Timtex™, S-A-S 2, and fabrics of the same size. If you are making the animal print box, Fabric 2 in the following charts corresponds to the tiger print and Fabric 3 to the black.

Chart 1

Item	#	Size
Timtex™	1	4-3/8"x22"
	1	1-1/2"x22"
24" S-A-S 2	2	4-3/8"x24"
-OR-		
12" S-A-S 2	1	12-1/2"x12"
	1	6-1/2"x12"
Fabric 2	1	4-3/8"x45"
Fabric 3	1	3-1/4"x 45"

Chart 2

Item	#	Size
Timtex		
Flaps (G)	1	4-3/8"x12-1/2"
Front & Back	2	4-3/8"x3-1/4"
Bottom	1	4-3/8"x1-1/2"
Sides	2	3-1/4"x1-1/2"
24" S-A-S 2		
Flaps (G)	2	4-3/8"x12-1/2"
Front & Back	4	4-3/8"x3-1/4"
Bottom	2	4-3/8"x1-1/2"
Sides	4	3-1/4"x1-1/2"
-OR-		
12' S-A-S 2		
Flaps (G)	2	4-3/8"x12-1/2"
Bottom	2	4-3/8"x1-1/2"
Sides	4	3-1/4"x1-1/2"
Front & Back	4	4-3/8"x3-1/4"
Fabric 2		
Flaps (G)	2	4-3/8"x12-1/2"
Bottom	1	4-3/8"x1-1/2"
Fabric 3		
Front & Back	4	4-3/8"x3-1/4"
Bottom	1	4-3/8"x1-1/2"
Sides	4	3-1/4"x1-1/2"

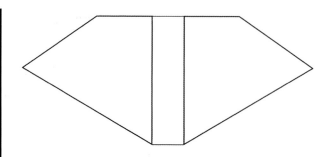

⌘ Step 2. Sandwiching
(see page 20)

Layer pieces of Timtex™, fabrics and S-A-S 2. Steam iron each of the stacks you have made from step 1. Each piece should have the same fabric on each side except the bottom. The bottom should have fabric 2 on one side and fabric 3 on the other.

✂ Step 3. Cutting (see page 18)

Trim pieces down to the sizes listed in Chart 3. Do not forget, for the Flaps you will need to cut two pieces from the letter side of your template and two from the (R) reverse side.

Chart 3

Item	#	Size
Front	1	3" x 4-1/8"
Back	1	3" x 4-1/8"
Sides	2	1-1/4" x 3"
Flaps	2	G
Flaps	2	G-R
Bottom	1	1-1/4" x 4-1/8"

⌘ Step 4. Satin Stitch
(see page 22)

- Satin stitch the sides and top of the Back and Front. Satin stitch these to the 4-1/8" sides of the bottom. Fabric 2 needs to be on the inside of the box. There is no need to satin stitch a second time on the seams joining the Front and Back to the Bottom at this time. Set this unit aside.

- Satin stitch the Flaps to the Side pieces. Be sure you line up the tops very carefully (see drawing).

- Satin stitch around the entire outside of these newly joined pieces except the small 1-1/4" section at the bottom of the side piece.

- Satin stitch the Side/Flaps unit to the Bottom.

- With the outside of the box facing up, stitch around the entire Bottom, with a bit wider satin stitch.

⌘ Step 5. Cross-Over Construction B (see page 24)

This is the smallest project using the cross-over construction technique and is therefore the most challenging to fit under the foot of your sewing machine. It is also not going to require the same strength as the larger bags. So, if you find it is too difficult to sew the top edges with your machine, you have some options. First, you could just glue the pieces together. Secondly, you could glue the pieces together and then hand tack the top edges making it a bit sturdier. Don't forget that the Timtex™ is very forgiving and you can iron the piece after you are finished. A small block of wood inside the box makes ironing much easier.

⌘ Step 6. Embellishments
(see page 91)

Dressing up the finished box is the most fun! A few beads strung at the point of the inverted V is easy to do. Be sure your thread and needle can fit through the holes in your beads. Thread the needle with enough thread to go through the beads twice and have enough thread left to tie off. Knot the thread and hide it under the flap. Thread your beads on the thread and place a seed bead at the end. Thread back through the other beads (see drawing) and take a stitch into the fabric. Secure the beads snuggly at the top and hide the second knot under the flap. Do the same to the other side.

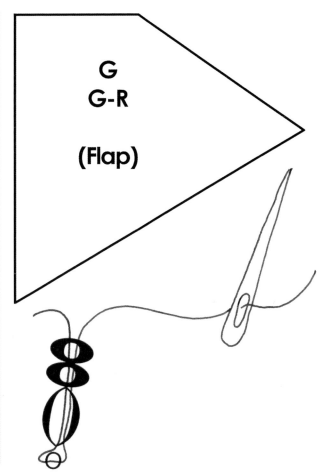

G
G-R

(Flap)

⌘ Handles & Hardware

The tools listed below are used to attach the handles and the hardware. These supplies do not appear in the Basic Supplies at the beginning of the book nor in the individual project supply lists.

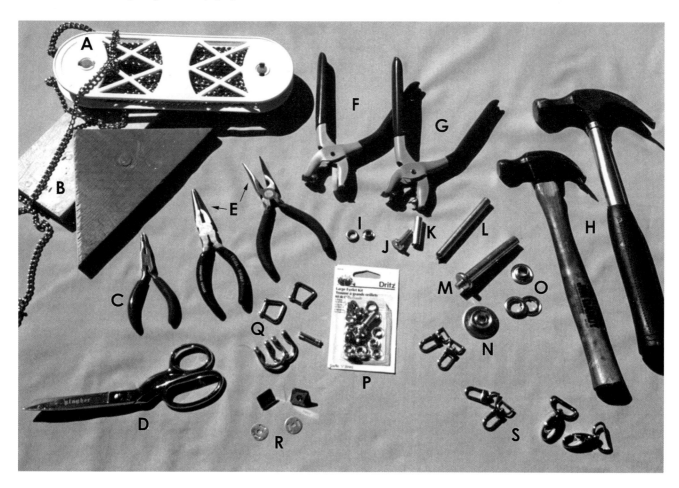

A - Chain
B - Block of Wood
C - Shaft Cutter
D - Scissors
E - Long Nosed Pliers
F - Dritz Grommet Pliers
G - Dritz Eyelet Pliers
H - Small and Large Hammers
I - Eyelets
J - Eyelet Setting Tool

K - Eyelet Tool
L - Punch
M - Grommet Tool
N - Grommet Stand
O - Grommets
P - Eyelets and Setting Kit
Q - Horseshoe Hooks
R - Magnetic Clasps
S - Chain Clasps

Not Shown
- Small Phillips Screwdriver
- Small Flat (or Slotted) Screwdriver

A bamboo handle may look adorable on the Evening Take-Out Bag. But the bamboo handle is not functional for this bag, as it would make opening the lid of the bag very difficult. Changing handle types from one bag to another is one way to personalize your bag. It is important that the handle chosen not only looks great but also is functional and is capable of supporting the weight the bag was designed to carry. Another point to consider is the stability of the bag. Read through this section of the book before making any changes to the projects and prior to beginning the cross-over construction step of your bag. It will help you decide if the desired handle type works well with the bag you are making and if you are willing to do the work it takes to apply a different handle to your bag. Most handles are fairly easy to install. However, if the eyelets/grommets are placed deep into a piece, installation will be a bit more difficult.

⌘ Eyelet/Grommet Installation

Adding stability is an important aspect to consider when deciding on which handle type to use. Eyelet/grommet installation adds a great deal of stability if it is done correctly. Grommets are larger and may be the better choice for some bags. Bags that are going to get daily use or be used to carry heavy weight need the greatest stability. The installation procedure for eyelets or grommets is very similar. Stability is increased if the eyelet/grommet is placed through the flaps when possible. Eyelets are not as deep and you will encounter some difficulty when penetrating the two layers of the textile sandwich. Another consideration is the depth at which the eyelet/grommet insertion will be placed. The eyelet/grommet pliers are not able to reach much deeper than an inch from the edge of a piece. It is still possible to place them deep into a piece but the procedure is a bit more difficult. Instructions on eyelet/grommet insertion with a hammer and tool will be given later in this section.

⌘ Step 1. Placement

Determine the placement for the eyelet/grommet. Placement is indicated within the pattern for each bag. Mark the spot by placing the deep half of the eyelet/grommet on the exterior of the bag and tracing it onto the fabric.

⌘ Step 2. Cutting the Hole

There are a number of ways this step can be accomplished. If you have eyelet/grommet pliers follow the manufactures instructions. Some of the pliers I have tried are not able to cut through two layers of textile sandwich. The Dritz eyelet pliers are able to punch through the double sandwich but the hole is not big enough to push the post through with only one punch. Multiple punches will do the job or provide an entry for scissor. If you don't have eyelet or grommet pliers, a very inexpensive tool called an eyelet setting tool can be used. It is easy. With a block of wood under the bag, place the sharp end of the eyelet setting tool over the traced hole and strike the tool with a hammer. This will leave a star shaped hole in the textile sandwich. Scissors can easily penetrate the sandwich through this hole to facilitate cutting out the previously traced area.

⌘ Step 3. Inserting and Crimping the Eyelet/Grommet

Press the post side of the eyelet/grommet piece through the hole from the exterior of the bag. Be sure the fabric completely clears t he post. Place the washer or flat portion of the eyelet/grommet dome-side out over the post. Press the units firmly together with your fingers. The washer and post must stay aligned when crimping the post. When using the eyelet pliers, place the punch side of the pliers through the washer side of the eyelet and tightly squeeze the handles. When using grommet pliers, the large end of the plastic platform needs to be rotated to the front of the pliers before placing the prepared sandwich into the pliers. Place the grommet into the platform with the post up. Be sure the washer is properly aligned and squeeze the handles tightly.

⌘ Eyelet/Grommet Installation with Hammer and Punch

There are times when eyelets or grommets are placed deep into piece where the pliers are unable to reach. Although more difficulty can be encountered when installing eyelets/grommets in these places, it can be accomplished successfully. Most hardware stores have eyelet/grommet tool kits if you are unable to locate them in your favorite fabric store. These kits are very similar no matter what brand you choose. A very hard surface is required on which to work. I use a block of wood for this type of eyelet installation.

⌘ Step 1. Placement and Cutting

Mark the placement by tracing the hole of the eyelet/grommet onto the bag in the desired location. Most grommet tool kits have a punch in them. I have found it is more difficult to cut the textile sandwich with the grommet punch than with scissors. A very inexpensive eyelet setting tool can be used. With a block of wood under the bag, place the sharp end of the eyelet setting tool over the traced hole and strike the tool with a hammer. This will leave a star shaped hole in the textile sandwich. Scissors can easily penetrate the sandwich through this hole to facilitate cutting out the previously traced area. The more accurate and clean the hole is, the easier it will be to finish the installation.

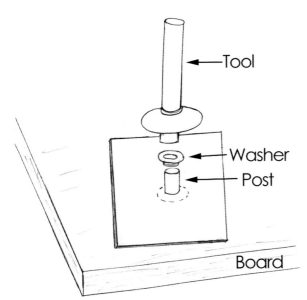

Tool

Washer

Post

Board

⌘ Step 2. Inserting the Eyelet/Grommet

Press the eyelet/grommet piece that has the post through the hole from the exterior of the bag. Be sure the fabric completely clears the post. Place the washer, or flat portion of the eyelet/grommet, dome-side up over the post. Press the units firmly together with your fingers. The washer and post must stay aligned when crimping the post (see drawing).

⌘ Step 3. Inserting & Crimping the Eyelet/Grommet

Eyelets are different than grommets in this step. For eyelets, place the project on a block of wood with the post facing up. Place the large end of the tool (the flange) over the washer and strike it firmly with a hammer. This should crimp the post over the washer. It may be necessary to strike the tool more than once. Rotate the project between each hammer strike (see drawing).

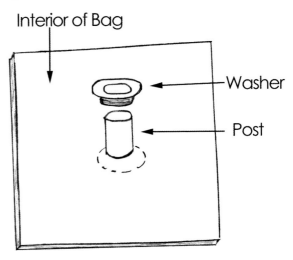

Interior of Bag

Washer

Post

Grommets are much heavier and need the hardest striking surface possible. Place the metal stand on the hard surface. Fit the prepared project from step 2, washer-side down, into the stand.

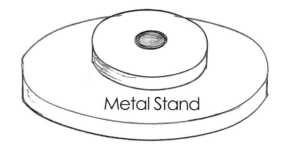
Metal Stand

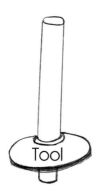
Tool

The post should be facing up. Slide the tip of the tool (see drawing) into the hole of the post and strike firmly with the hammer. Because the grommet installation requires a harder striking surface, I use a cement floor or block. I also use a fairly large hammer for the grommet installation.

⌘ Scrunchie Handle Attachment With Eyelets/Grommets (Red Evening Take-Out Bag)

This handle can be adjusted for use on any bag. Eyelets will hold the handles on a small bag. They can penetrate a single layer of textile sandwich along with the handle ends. Use grommets for a stronger handle installation. A grommet can penetrate 2 layers of textile sandwich and the handle. Grommet installed handles can also hold a good deal of weight.

- Mark the spot for cutting the holes on the exterior of the bag. Also mark a spot for the hole in the center of the 1/2" end of the handle. Trace the post of the eyelet/grommet for marking the holes. Using an eyelet setting tool, puncture the marked spots on the bag and handles.

- Cut the holes out with sharp scissors.

- Place the post through the handle and the exterior of the bag and follow the crimping instructions for Eyelet/Grommet Installation with a Hammer and Punch.

- Select the button for covering the eyelet/grommet. It is best to choose a button with a shank. Cover the back of the button with fabric glue. Put the shank through the eyelet/grommet hole and fill the hole from the inside of the bag with fabric glue. Lay the bag on its side so the glue can dry over-night. Repeat the button attachment at the other end of the handle.

⌘ Horseshoe Hook Handle Attachment

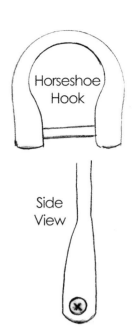

Horseshoe Hook

Side View

This is one of the easiest handle attachments. You will need either a small flat (slotted) screwdriver or a small Phillips screwdriver. Check the end of the screw at the base of the horseshoe hook. Remove the screw by simply unscrewing it with the appropriate screwdriver and slipping it out of the hole. While removing the screws take note which side of the hook receives the threads of the screw. This will be the side that needs to be pushed through the tabs toward the center of the bag. After pushing the hooks through the tabs, line up the hole in the handle with the holes of the horseshoe loop and thread the screw through. With the appropriate screwdriver, tighten the screw. Be careful not to strip the threads.

⌘ D-Ring Attachment

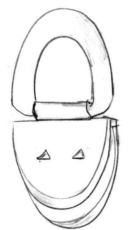

A D-Ring is simply a metal ring shaped like the letter "D". Its opposing side is two solid D-shaped metal pieces (see drawing). One side of this solid portion has teeth. The other side is smooth. The D-ring can be attached at any desirable place on the bag providing a convenient place to clip your keys. It is simple to attach. Slide the textile sandwich into the open solid side of the ring and tap it lightly with a hammer. I cover the top of the D-ring with a scrap of Timtex™ and set the bag on a block of wood so that I avoid marring the surface of the D-ring. D-rings come in many sizes. If the large D-rings are used, they can make handle attachment a breeze. Simply decide on the desired placement and clip the D-rings in place as described above and attach a chain into the open portion of the D-ring and your handle is finished.

⌘ Chain Attachment

Measure the chain and cut it to the desired length. Use two pair of needle nosed pliers to spread one link open by twisting each side in the opposite direction. If two lengths are needed, cut the second length and lay the pieces side by side to check them for exact size. Thread the chain through the eyelet/grommet hole that has already been inserted and connect the chain back together. This is accomplished by slipping the open link through the two end links of your threaded chain and gently twisting that link back into its original position.

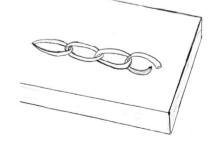

⌘ Magnetic Clasps

There are a number of brands of magnetic clasps. Some are round and some are square but all are installed in the same way and it is so easy. Proper placement is critical and there are a couple of tricks. Placement for clasps on the *Cross-Over Hand Bag* is explained in the pattern. Placement for the clasps on the *Evening Take-Out Bag* is as follows. It is best to install the clasp on the front of the bag first since aligning the clasp on the Front Closure Flap is easier. The clasp on the front needs to be placed in the center and about 2" down from the top. The prongs need to penetrate two layers of textile sandwich so the 2" measurement is an approximation. DON'T place the prongs through three layers of textile sandwich. See the drawing to help with the placement.

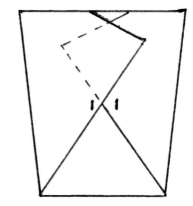

After the clasp has been placed in the front of the bag, close the bag top and mark the spot on the Front Closure Flap that aligns with the lower clasp. This is accomplished most easily by snapping the clasps together and marking where the prongs hit the Front Closure Flap.

Gather the following supplies needed for the installation; a small hammer, a block of wood, needle nosed pliers and a small flat (slotted) screwdriver.

- Cut the holes for the prongs by placing the bag on the block of wood and line the end of the screwdriver up on a mark indicated for placement of the clasp. Tap the screwdriver with the hammer and the hole should be lined up perfectly through both layers of textile sandwich. Repeat for the second hole.

- Slip the prongs through the holes.

- Slide the washer over the prongs and fold them down toward the center of the washer using needle nosed pliers.

- Set the clasp face down on the block of wood and tap the folded prongs gently to secure the clasp.

- Repeat this process for the other half of the clasp.

⌘ Embellishments

Once the project is sewn and the wrinkles are pressed out, it is time to individualize and embellish! Make it fun, sassy, sophisticated, elegant or whimsical; you are the creator/ designer. Here are some ideas to start those creative juices flowing. If your project is going to get regular or rough use, be sure your embellishments are attached accordingly.

⌘ Embroidery

Embroidery, as mentioned before, is best stitched before sandwiching. Planning ahead for this is imperative. The easiest way to add embroidery to a project is to embroider the fabric before cutting the project out. Cut a larger piece of fabric than is required for the piece on which you wish to place the design. This will allow for careful positioning of the design. Place the design exactly where you wish to have it appear on the finished project and cut the piece out.

⌘ Quilting

Quilting also requires some planning ahead. It is not required for structural integrity but does add that little something extra. I don't recommend hand quilting as the thickness of the sandwich makes it very difficult. There are a couple of ways to approach quilting these bags. First, quilting each piece before sewing the pieces together is the easiest to handle. However, if your quilt design calls for the pattern to flow from one piece to an attached piece then sewing the pieces together first would be the best way to go. Either way, the bag needs to be quilted before assembly. Metallic threads, contrasting thread or even same color thread can add a delicate and refined texture to the bag. All of the above are great additions.

⌘ Decorative Stitching

Depending on the machine used, decorative stitching can be added before or after the fusing process. Some simple designs are fine to add after the bag has been sewn together but before the construction phase. I would suggest that you try the decorative stitch on a piece of sandwich, even if that means making a small piece of sandwich on which to experiment prior to beginning a project. Very dense decorative stitches should be treated in the same fashion as embroidery.

⌘ Buttons

It is a bit difficult to hand-sew through the sandwich especially if more than one layer needs to be sewn through. All of the buttons seen in this book have been glued on with liquid fabric glue after the button shaft has been removed. Following are a number of ideas for your consideration.

Covered buttons (often labeled "Cover Buttons") add a classic tailored look to any project. They come in many different sizes and the instructions on the package are easy to follow. After covering them, remove the shank by cutting it off with long nosed pliers or purchase a shaft cutter which is very inexpensive and easy to use.

Buttons with holes are cute but need to have the thread sewn through the holes before gluing them on to the bag. If these buttons are going to be placed on a single layer of sandwich, it is not too difficult to sew through a single layer. I still prefer to glue them in place after running thread through the holes.

Buttons with a shaft are often decorative and sometimes very whimsical. They provide a great range of choice. As mentioned in the cover buttons section above, the shaft needs to be removed first with either long-nosed pliers or a shaft cutter. Use your imagination. The same button in different sizes can line the angle of the cross-over flap for a very attractive look. One button on each corner of the bottom can add a little protection and decrease the wear and tear on the bottom of the bag. There are just so many ways buttons can be used to decorate! Use them any place they look good.

⌘ Beads, Trim, Feathers, Chain and Old Jewelry

Beads, trim, feathers, chain and old jewelry are all great ways to jazz up a bag.

- Beaded trim or separate beads threaded to dangle can be added at any spot on a project. They can be sewn or glued on with liquid fabric glue. Instructions on how to add single lines of threaded beads can be found in the Cozy Coasters pattern (see page).

- Feathers or feather boas can be added with glue or sewn into place.

- Ribbons tied into bows or made into runners and sewn or glued into place can add softness to any bag.

- Chain or jewelry can add that special pizzazz to your project. This is a great way to reuse a piece of jewelry you like or has special meaning but you no longer care to wear.

The most important thing to remember about embellishing is to let your imagination run wild and to have lots of fun with it!

⌘ Sew What Now ? ! ?
(Trouble Shooting)

It is impossible to address everything that could potentially happen while making these projects. I will give suggestions on how to handle the most frequently occurring problems.

⌘ Problem:

The fabric separates from the Timtex™.

⌘ Solution:

It is simply a matter of spending more time on the fusing process. Be sure to follow the manufactures instructions for the fusible web you have chosen. Some fusible webs can loose their fusing properties by overheating. Those products are not the best for these projects since you will want to iron them at different times throughout the entire process. For the next project make sure that the fusible web you choose won't lose the fusing properties by overheating.

⌘ Problem:

After ironing the fabric to the Timtex ™, the sandwich looks dimpled.

⌘ Solution:

This problem is only rectified by prevention. Timtex™ is a synthetic as are all the thick interfacings of which I am aware. With this fact in mind, while the cotton fabric and the S-A-S 2 can handle a hot blast of steam, the Timtex™ needs to be treated a little more gently. Take a little more time fusing and don't use hot blasts of steam. If your iron cannot be turned down to a light steam, then iron with a dry iron and spritz the sandwich with a fine spray of water from a spray bottle before ironing.

⌘ Problem:

When satin stitching a seam, it is difficult to see where the two pieces come together, especially when both pieces have the same fabric.

⌘ Solution:

Chalk the edge of one of the pieces before beginning to sew. It may also be appropriate to make a color marking on the center of the foot if it doesn't have one. This will make it much easier to see where the stitching line needs to be positioned while you are sewing.

⌘ Problem:

The needle keeps breaking.

⌘ Solution:

It is easy to push or pull the textile sandwich as you are sewing without being aware of the force being applied. When the needle is in the down position, pushing or pulling will often break the needle. Another possibility is that the wrong needle is in the machine for the type of sewing you are doing. I recommend using a 60/8 or 70/10 Microtex sharp needle.

⌘ Problem:

Threads pull through to the opposite side of the sandwich.

⌘ Solution:

The tensions on your machine often need to be adjusted when sewing with a thicker layer of material. Before changing any tension, check the threading of both the top and bobbin. If the thread is pulling through to the top, the bobbin tension needs adjustment. If the thread is pulling through to the underside, the tension adjustment needs to be made on the top. Using different colors of thread on the top and in the bobbin will require careful and possible constant attention to your tension adjustments. This is one of the reasons I prefer using the same color thread in the bobbin as on top.

⌘ Problem:

A lump forms in the satin stitch especially when turning the corner.

⌘ Solution:

Slightly lift the presser foot at the corners. This can be done in a number of ways. Sew two pieces of Timtex™ together and make it a part of your sewing kit. Place it under the back of the foot to help relieve some of the pressure. Often a small plastic gadget comes with the machine to use in the same way as the double layer of Timtex™. (PICTURE) Many machines have the capability of programming in a lighter foot pressure. Check the manual and follow the instructions. Manually pushing the textile sandwich gently can sometimes work. I don't recommend it as this can cause the needle to break or leave a gap in the stitching after the lump is cleared.

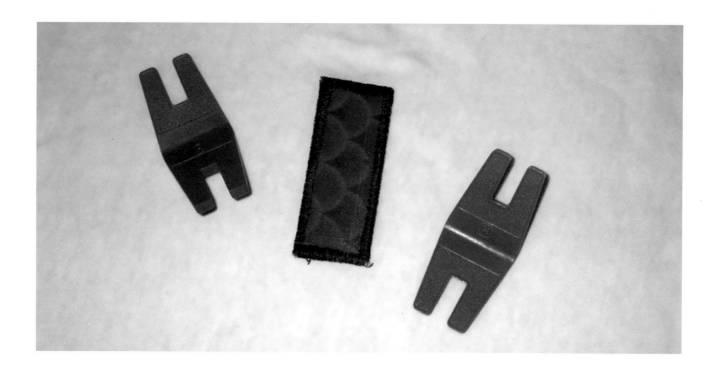

⌘ Problem:

The project is finished but the fabric next to the satin stitch looks frayed.

⌘ Solution:

This is often a problem with using the incorrect needle size, type or one that has simply gotten dull. The correct needle for the next project will be needed. But for the damaged project, camouflage is the solution. A string of beads glued over the seams or some other decorative innovation will work wonders. Use some form of liquid fray stopper before applying the camouflage.

⌘ Problem:

Excess glue has gotten on the bag where it wasn't intended.

⌘ Solution:

Remove as much of the excess glue as you can with a thin piece of cardboard. Don't rub it in by trying to scrub it off. Lay a piece of brown paper bag over the glue and iron it. Lift the paper while it is still warm and the glue should come off on the paper. Repeat the steps if all the glue doesn't come off the first time. Be sure to use a new piece of paper bag each time so the glue is not ironed back onto the bag.

⌘ Problem:

Inadvertently the magnetic clasp was not installed before the front and back of the piece was sandwiched.

⌘ Solution:

It is not really a big problem as the back of the clasp is on the inside of the bag. However, if you want to cover the back of the clasp, just cut a small square of the same fabric used at the site of the clasp back and fold the edges under. Glue the fabric square in place over the clasp back with liquid fabric glue.

⌘ About the Author

Jeanne Perrine was born in Illinois, raised in Michigan, and has lived in Georgia, Utah, Germany and two tours in Alaska giving her a wide and varied scope of cultures to draw from. She now resides with her husband, Merle, in the Chicago suburbs. She is a wife and mother of two grown children, a Registered Nurse, and teaches quilting, sewing and stained glass to all who will sit still long enough. Daughter Trilisa is a Doctoral candidate at the University of Chicago and son Luke makes his home in Alaska.

Creativity has always been an important part of Jeanne's life. A major component of expressing that creativity has been the medium of fabric. She has sewn from the time she could reach both the treadle and the machine top at the same time. As a child she would make "creations" out of the most unusual items. Not all of them were beautiful but they were all unique. Not being able to read pattern instructions at the age of five didn't stop her from designing great outfits for her dolls or herself. Granted, the clothing didn't always fit. But let's face it, it's all about the journey and the learning process anyway. Figuring out how to construct an article out of an idea and incorporating the design lines, textures and colors has always been a joy to her.

When Jeanne is asked, "How long have you been sewing?" Her response usually goes something like this. "I can't remember the time when the need to be creative wasn't a part of me. That creativity routinely manifests itself in sewing." Jeanne has been sewing since she was a little girl under the tutelage of her mother. She's studied color and design on her own for some thirty-five years. She has received first place and "Best of Show" awards in stained glass work in statewide competitions on numerous occasions. As a teenager she took honors for 4-H sewing ensembles and modeling her creations. She spends more time now in teaching and developing patterns.

"Married to an Air Force pilot, I was afforded the opportunity to live in several states and countries and to visit many more on an extended basis. This was great for experiencing different types of artistic expressions and cultures." Exposure to each culture's distinctively different art forms inspired Jeanne's development of her own eclectic style of expression.

Teaching is a natural progression for Jeanne. People often ask her, "How did you make that?" Regardless of whether we're talking about glass, pottery, fabric, or some combination of them all, the response goes something like this. "Get a couple of friends together and we'll hold a class and I'll show you how." That sort of thing has happened more times than can be counted. Near the end of many such impromptu class sessions Jeanne often gets comments like, "You should write a book about this." All the prompting has brought her to this point. Finally, here is the book. Do enjoy making these projects and use it to stimulate and invigorate your own creative juices. "I believe we all have a creative bent just waiting to be expressed." Have a great time!

⌘ Sources

Most of the tools and materials needed for the projects in this book are available in your local quilt, fabric or craft shop. Try the following sources if you are unable to find supplies.

⌘ Timtex™

(for wholesale orders or to direct you to a retail outlet near you)
Timber Lane Press
24350 N. Rimrock Road
Hayden, ID 83835
800-752-3353 - wholesale only
208-765-3353 - inquiries
Email: qltblox@earthlink.net

⌘ Steam-A-Seam 2 ®

(for questions about S-A-S 2 and many other products)
The Warm Company™
954 East Union Street
Seattle, WA 98122
800-234-WARM
Fax: 206-320-0974
www.warmcompany.com
Call The Warm Company's 800 number above for a free sample of Steam-A-Seam 2.

⌘ Rulers, Pliers and Accessories

Prym-Dritz Corp.
P.O. Box 5028
Spartanburg, SC 29304
www.Dritz.com

⌘ Other Supplies

Judy's Quilt 'N' Sew
290 South State Street
Hampshire, IL 60140
847-683-4739
www.friendshipstar.com

⌘ Books Directly from the Author

Jeanne L. Perrine
www.JeannesEclecticDesigns.com
jeanneperrine@gmail.com